Prophetic PRAYER

BREAKING GROUND, SPIRITUAL BIRTHING, AND DECREE

COLETTE TOACH

www.ami-bookshop.com

Prophetic Prayer
Breaking Ground, Spiritual Birthing, and Decree

ISBN-13: 978-1-62664-226-3

Other formats of this book:
eBook ISBN: 978-1-62664-227-0
Kindle ISBN: 978-1-62664-228-7
iBook ISBN: 978-1-62664-229-4

Copyright © 2020 by Apostolic Movement International, LLC
All rights reserved
5663 Balboa Ave #416,
San Diego,
California 92111,
United States of America

1st Printing July 2020

Published by **Apostolic Movement International, LLC**
E-mail Address: admin@ami-bookshop.com
Web Address: www.ami-bookshop.com

All rights reserved under International Copyright Law.
Contents may not be reproduced in whole or in part in any form without the express written consent of the publisher.

Unless specified, all Scripture references taken from the New King James Version®. Copyright © 1982 by Thomas Nelson. Used by permission. All rights reserved.

CONTENTS

1 - Breaking Ground: Prophetic Prayer in Motion 9
    Breaking Ground 10
    People and Circumstances Need to Be Aligned 11
    The Ground We Break 13

2 - Breaking Ground: Preparing the Hearts of God's People 17
    Power to Change the Heart of Man 21
    God Will Begin at Home 23
    The Process 26

3 - Breaking Ground: Preparing Circumstances 29
    The Fivefold Ministry at Work 29
    Pray Always 31

4 - Breaking Ground: Preparing for the Vision 35
    That Pesky Prayer Burden 37
    Prophetic Authority 37
    Making Bricks – Putting Jesus on the Throne of Circumstances 38
    Are We Ready for Rain? 42

5 - Breaking Ground: Steps 1-5 45
    How to Identify When to Break Ground 45

Step 1: Pray Without Ceasing 47
Step 2: Keep Focused 49
Step 3: Pray in the Spirit and With Understanding . 52
Step 4: Strengthen Yourself in Faith – Use the Word
.... 54
Step 5: Bind the Enemy 57
Do Not Forget to Praise! 59
6 - Owning Your Piece of the Wall 63
Your Piece of the Wall 65
7 - Wall Building 101 71
WARNING! Watch for Spiritual Blockages 77
Pick up Your Trowel 78
Pray the Vision Through 79
Identify When God Switches Gears 81
8 - Entering the Throne Room 83
9 - Spiritual Birthing From the Throne Room 87
Reaching Beyond Prophetic Ministry 88
Feeling What God Feels 89
The Heart of the Father 90
The Travailing Process 91
The Purpose of Spiritual Birthing 93
Paying the Price Others Will Not Pay 94
10 - Spiritual Birthing: The Travailing Process 97
The Birthing Experience 97

    Putting Things Into Order 99

    Birthing for Others 101

    My Personal Experience 102

    The Fruit of Today From Yesterday's Travail 104

11 - Spiritual Birthing: The Steps of the Travailing Process 107

    What Spiritual Birthing Looks Like 110

    1. Intense Emotions 110

    2. Feeling It Physically 111

    3. Tears and Loss of Words 113

    4. The Baby Is Born 114

    5. Decree and Warfare 116

    6. Prophecy – Keeping the Midwives Motivated .. 117

12 - Spiritual Warfare From the Throne Room 119

    Keeping Your Baby Safe 120

    The Enemy Will Be Revealed 122

    Build up, Tear Down 122

13 - Decree and Prophecy From the Throne Room .. 127

    You Are Positioned 127

    The Power of Release 129

    The Nitty-Gritty of Decree 130

    The Equipping Power of Decree 131

    Now… Step Out and Prophesy, Prophet! 132

    Be Accountable! 134

- The Prophet's Passion 137
- Prophetic Prayer: 138
- BONUS - Practical Do's and Don'ts of Prophetic Prayer 139
  - DO NOT Use Prophetic Prayer as a Personal Prayer Time 139
  - DO Stand in AUTHORITY, Not in Hysterical Shouting 140
  - DO Stand in the Mantle of Anointing 142
  - DO When Praying With Others, Jump in One Another's Rivers 143
  - DO NOT Pray Fast and Fumble. Speak Clearly 144
  - DO NOT Quit When the Lull Comes 146
  - DO STOP Once the Decree Has Gone Out 146
  - DO NOT Use the Word Against the Lord 147
  - DO NOT Just Quote Scriptures and Call That Prayer 148
  - DO NOT Be Apologetic for Your Revelation 149
  - DO NOT Stop to Share All Your Revelations 151
  - DO NOT Preach a Sermon 152
  - The Prophet: Armed and Dangerous 153
- About the Author 155
- Other Books by Colette Toach 156
  - Persistent Prayer 156
  - Strategies of War 157

   Prophetic Anointing 157
Further Recommendations by the Author 158
   AMI Prophetic School: 158
   AMI Pastor Teacher School: 159
   AMI Campus: 160
Reach out! 161
Bibliography 162

1
BREAKING GROUND: PROPHETIC PRAYER IN MOTION

Now, before I get into my first subject entitled, *Breaking Ground*, let me introduce myself. If you have read any of my teachings, you know that I like to keep things practical, real, and nicely laid out. Organization makes me feel settled. Connecting with people like you, is my happy place. I tend to run my mouth off too much, and so I got a solid burn or two, from being just a tad too "real" with my perspective on the prophet.

I wrote an entire series for the prophet-in-training called, *The Prophetic Field Guide Series*[i].

To clarify: This book... is not that series.

This book takes you by the hand as you enter prophetic office, and look around wondering, "Now what?" It's one thing to go through the process of becoming a prophet and another to stand in office. So, I am picking up from where I left off in the field guide series to give you the tools you need for the battlefield in front of you.

I am assuming that you are a prophet in office. I am assuming that you already know how to pray, ground. Until the hearts of God's people are prepared, you are not going anywhere with that revelation.

What you feel in the spirit and what you do with it is the dividing line between intent and the manifestation of God's plan in this earth.

You could keep telling others what you see and feel, or you could pick up a trowel and begin to build. You do that with the one tool God has spent a lot of time proving in the fire – your mouth!

The words you release into this earth through prayer and prophecy hold the power to take what God intends to do and cause it to be made manifest. The first step the Lord always takes, is to get His people on board.

WHAT YOU FEEL IN THE SPIRIT AND WHAT YOU DO WITH IT IS THE DIVIDING LINE BETWEEN INTENT AND THE MANIFESTATION OF GOD'S PLAN IN THIS EARTH.

Before Moses went before Pharaoh, he visited the Israelites first. God visited Noah before the flood came. He encountered Samuel long before He established King David on the throne and put the Kingdom of Israel in place.

The Lord won't establish any plan in this earth without knocking on man's door first. Once His people are in line, then they can be equipped to build. Solomon had to be born and raised by a king to construct a

You should praise God that you are not Moses. It could be worse... so much worse. Does that give you a little perspective?

The good thing is that we do not need to wait for 40 years, because we have something that Moses did not. We have the indwelling of the Holy Spirit. We have the spirit of God within us that doesn't only give us the revelation but also empowers us to speak it forth.

> *HENCE WHY WE HAVE THE FIVEFOLD MINISTRY IN THE NEW TESTAMENT, AND WHY GOD PUT THIS MANTLE ON YOUR SHOULDERS AND HIS AUTHORITY IN YOUR BELLY.*

Hence why we have the fivefold ministry in the New Testament, and why God put this mantle on your shoulders and His authority in your belly.

It was so that you might speak God's word out and cause these things to come to pass.

Softening Hard Hearts

It is time that the hard hearts of God's people are softened. I promise that it is not going to happen by standing behind the pulpit, condemning people and churches that are not getting it right.

You will only become discouraged if you try to lead worship by telling the congregation that it is time for them to stand up and worship God because if they don't, they will be cursed (Been in one of those meetings. Not keen to sit through a repeat!).

You think that if you publicly correct leaders that are out of line, the masses will flock to you. You will get the masses alright... all the masses that are bitter against leaders. I am not convinced that this is the kind of move that God intends for His Church.

This approach does not work. That is like Moses whipping that Egyptian and expecting everybody to love him. It did not go well. He thought that he would step in and tell them not to fight amongst themselves - giving them a bit of a correction. It did not go down well.

Their hearts were ready when God made their hearts ready.

It is only the spirit of God who understands the things of God. The spirit of man cannot comprehend it. The carnal mind cannot comprehend the things of the spirit. Only the spirit that God has put in man can understand (1 Corinthians 2:14).

You cannot force yourself on someone else's spirit. However, good news - the Holy Spirit has taken hold of the spirit of man in the church, because they submitted themselves to Him.

Blood-bought, born again believers have their spirits influenced by the Holy Spirit.

"Oh, my goodness! That means that you do not have to be the Holy Spirit!"

1
BREAKING GROUND: PROPHETIC PRAYER IN MOTION

Now, before I get into my first subject entitled, *Breaking Ground*, let me introduce myself. If you have read any of my teachings, you know that I like to keep things practical, real, and nicely laid out. Organization makes me feel settled. Connecting with people like you, is my happy place. I tend to run my mouth off too much, and so I got a solid burn or two, from being just a tad too "real" with my perspective on the prophet.

I wrote an entire series for the prophet-in-training called, *The Prophetic Field Guide Series*[i].

To clarify: This book… is not that series.

This book takes you by the hand as you enter prophetic office, and look around wondering, "Now what?" It's one thing to go through the process of becoming a prophet and another to stand in office. So, I am picking up from where I left off in the field guide series to give you the tools you need for the battlefield in front of you.

I am assuming that you are a prophet in office. I am assuming that you already know how to pray, intercede, and minister inner healing to one degree or another.

I am also assuming that you are adept at putting your flesh on the cross and dumping your preconceived ideas. Hey... you and I both know how much shaking you have gone through to get to this stage of your journey. So, let us neither underestimate the authority that God has given to you nor your ability to use it.

Instead, let me point you in the right direction. Allow me to challenge you and provoke thought. Perhaps along the way you will gain a new perspective of your prophetic calling and will hopefully pick up a new weapon or two to deal some damage to the kingdom of darkness.

So, let's get to it, shall we? We are in for another roller coaster ride! There is no better way to experience it than to say, one...two...three... GO!

Breaking Ground

I had the opportunity to watch someone breaking ground. We were on a farm in Switzerland, at our ministry center, and they were preparing the field for their vegetable garden.

I was watching a young man preparing the ground for seed. He took a rake and fork and used them to break the ground up. What I found fascinating was that the ground was not even that hard.

The snow of winter had recently melted, so the ground was moist and soft. So, although there was a bit of a crust on the soil surface, it was pretty easy to break through.

Yet, as easy as this ground was, he still had to go over it again and again until the soil was prepared to receive the seeds. If they would have tried to put the seeds on the hard ground, either the birds would have come and eaten them, or the sun would have scorched them. They would never have had the opportunity to get their roots into the soil.

This time-consuming process is a very good picture of what you are called to do as a prophet, before God's will can be manifest in the earth.

So, as I share on the subject of prophetic prayer, I am talking about the kind of prayer that the prophet in office prays to get the job done. When God has a plan, He first reveals His secrets to the prophet.

I will share the process that you need to go through to cause God's plan to come to pass in the earth.

People and Circumstances Need to Be Aligned

When God reveals something to an apostle that plan, or pattern, needs to be made manifest in the earth.

How else is that plan or pattern going to come to pass practically?

It is going to involve people and circumstances being aligned. It is going to involve a lot more than just getting revelation. That is where you, as a prophet in office, come in. You need to begin breaking ground.

> ***Hosea 10:12*** *Sow for yourselves righteousness; reap in mercy; break up your fallow ground, for it is time to seek the Lord, till He comes and rains righteousness on you.*

Before you can reap in mercy, the rain needs to fall. Yet, before the rain can fall, the hard ground has to be broken up. That is your job as a prophet.

Until the hearts of God's people are ready for the vision, it cannot come to earth.

Until the circumstances are in line with the blueprint, it cannot be built. Let's say you get this great revelation of what God wants to do. That is like Ezra and Nehemiah getting a fantastic idea that they need to build a wall and a temple.

However, there is a time when you need to prepare and assemble the people in order to get the job done. The Lord gave them the pattern, but practically, they only began to build when the people were ready.

This is where you find your place. It is for you, as a prophet, to release those words in the spirit that bring people and circumstances in line.

> ***Jeremiah 1:10*** *See, I have this day set you over the nations and over the kingdoms,*
> *To root out and to pull down,*

*To destroy and to throw down,
To build and to plant."*

Along with the position that God has given you, comes a responsibility. The Lord told Jeremiah that he was set over nations and kingdoms. His work description was listed after. It is one thing to be positioned, and another to get the job done.

A vital aspect of your position is the responsibility to see God's work fulfilled in this earth: To build, to get people and circumstances in line,

> HAVE YOU BROKEN GROUND AND PREPARED THE HEARTS OF GOD'S PEOPLE FOR CHANGE?

and to see the vision through. This process is what I call "Breaking Ground."

The Ground We Break

Have you broken ground and prepared the hearts of God's people for change?

> ***Amos 3:7** Surely the Lord God does nothing, unless He reveals His secret to His servants the prophets.*

We are called to tear down, build up, uproot, and plant. However, when we think of this picture, our minds skip right to the finished product. Once you are done reading Jeremiah 1:10 you see the root already out, the building already built, and plants already planted!

The groundbreaking I am talking about is the transition phase between the "rooting out" and "planted."

The work you do as a prophet is everything in between the "tearing down" and the "building". You learned during your training (boot camp) how to receive revelation and the importance of hearing from God before you speak up. You were humbled, crushed, and then picked up. You learned when to speak up and when to sit down. However, you are in prophetic office now. This is where the rubber meets the road.

> THE GROUNDBREAKING I AM TALKING ABOUT IS THE TRANSITION PHASE BETWEEN THE "ROOTING OUT" AND "PLANTED."

Time to take things up a notch. Just getting revelation, or knowing what God wants to do in this earth is no longer good enough. Until the fervent prayer of the just avails much, that pattern and plan is not coming to pass.

Prayer and prophecy are the secret keys to unlocking the treasures of heaven, and the blueprint that God wants to see manifest in this earth.

You, as a prophet, have been given a very specific authority. You have a key that can open or close those doors. What have you done with your key today?

Getting revelation is not good enough. Having an impression in your spirit won't bring lasting change. Knowing what God wants is not good enough. Giving a prophetic word is not good enough. You need to break ground. Until the hearts of God's people are prepared, you are not going anywhere with that revelation.

What you feel in the spirit and what you do with it is the dividing line between intent and the manifestation of God's plan in this earth.

You could keep telling others what you see and feel, or you could pick up a trowel and begin to build. You do that with the one tool God has spent a lot of time proving in the fire – your mouth!

The words you release into this earth through prayer and prophecy hold the power to take what God intends to do and cause it to be made manifest. The first step the Lord always takes, is to get His people on board.

> *WHAT YOU FEEL IN THE SPIRIT AND WHAT YOU DO WITH IT IS THE DIVIDING LINE BETWEEN INTENT AND THE MANIFESTATION OF GOD'S PLAN IN THIS EARTH.*

Before Moses went before Pharaoh, he visited the Israelites first. God visited Noah before the flood came. He encountered Samuel long before He established King David on the throne and put the Kingdom of Israel in place.

The Lord won't establish any plan in this earth without knocking on man's door first. Once His people are in line, then they can be equipped to build. Solomon had to be born and raised by a king to construct a magnificent temple. So, you prophet, are to see this whole process through!

First though, let's get people ready for God's move!

---

[i] Toach, Colette. *Prophetic Field Guide Series*. Vol. 1-7. San Diego, California: Apostolic Movement International LLC, 2014 – 2016

2
BREAKING GROUND: PREPARING THE HEARTS OF GOD'S PEOPLE

> ***Jeremiah 4:3*** *For thus says the Lord to the men of Judah and Jerusalem: "Break up your fallow ground, and do not sow among thorns."*

You look at the state of the Church and you see how much change we need. You see the spirit of the world and the complacency. However, let's bring it even closer to home. Let's talk about the ministry that you are currently involved with.

Let's see where God has you at the moment. Where is He leading you in ministry? This applies to you whether you are in charge of the ministry or involved in someone else's ministry. What is the vision that God has given you?

You have this grand plan and exciting goal that you are running towards. However, listen to me very closely! There are two very good reasons why you need to break ground before moving to decree.

Reason #1 Firstly, the hearts of the people are not ready to receive the seed.

Reason #2 Secondly, the circumstances are not in alignment to allow the building to commence.

That is why you keep getting this call to prayer and why you keep feeling the same burden continually.

How many years did Moses spend in the wilderness before he was called to set the children of Israel free?

Israel had been enslaved for hundreds of years. You would think that by the end of that they would have been sick of being slaves. Moses rose up to slay that Egyptian and gave them an idea of what could happen if they just stood up for themselves. (Albeit in the flesh!)

Were they ready?

They scorned Moses and said, "Who do you think you are, coming to tell us what to do?" (Exodus 2:11-15)

Moses ran for his life. He went to the backside of the desert. After that, how long did it take for the hearts of God's people to be ready and for them to cry out for a deliverer, so that God could send Moses back?

40 years!

It took them that long to have their hearts prepared for change. Yet, you want to complain because you have been praying for four days, four weeks, or four months so far, and you still do not see change.

You should praise God that you are not Moses. It could be worse... so much worse. Does that give you a little perspective?

The good thing is that we do not need to wait for 40 years, because we have something that Moses did not. We have the indwelling of the Holy Spirit. We have the spirit of God within us that doesn't only give us the revelation but also empowers us to speak it forth.

> *HENCE WHY WE HAVE THE FIVEFOLD MINISTRY IN THE NEW TESTAMENT, AND WHY GOD PUT THIS MANTLE ON YOUR SHOULDERS AND HIS AUTHORITY IN YOUR BELLY.*

Hence why we have the fivefold ministry in the New Testament, and why God put this mantle on your shoulders and His authority in your belly.

It was so that you might speak God's word out and cause these things to come to pass.

Softening Hard Hearts

It is time that the hard hearts of God's people are softened. I promise that it is not going to happen by standing behind the pulpit, condemning people and churches that are not getting it right.

You will only become discouraged if you try to lead worship by telling the congregation that it is time for them to stand up and worship God because if they don't, they will be cursed (Been in one of those meetings. Not keen to sit through a repeat!).

You think that if you publicly correct leaders that are out of line, the masses will flock to you. You will get the masses alright... all the masses that are bitter against leaders. I am not convinced that this is the kind of move that God intends for His Church.

This approach does not work. That is like Moses whipping that Egyptian and expecting everybody to love him. It did not go well. He thought that he would step in and tell them not to fight amongst themselves - giving them a bit of a correction. It did not go down well.

Their hearts were ready when God made their hearts ready.

It is only the spirit of God who understands the things of God. The spirit of man cannot comprehend it. The carnal mind cannot comprehend the things of the spirit. Only the spirit that God has put in man can understand (1 Corinthians 2:14).

You cannot force yourself on someone else's spirit. However, good news - the Holy Spirit has taken hold of the spirit of man in the church, because they submitted themselves to Him.

Blood-bought, born again believers have their spirits influenced by the Holy Spirit.

"Oh, my goodness! That means that you do not have to be the Holy Spirit!"

Get That Revelation!

What you can do, however, is be used of God to speak forth the change and in so doing, move the hand of the Holy Spirit, so their hearts may begin to soften.

Who softened and hardened Pharaoh's heart and why was that heart softened and hardened?

It was because Moses acted in faith and obedience. As a result, the hand of God moved on Pharaoh's heart. When you act in obedience and break up the ground in prayer, the hand of God will move for you, too.

Not to worry, I am going to give you the steps 1-5 in the next couple of chapters. This way, you can follow the steps and be an efficient prophet in office, and we can start changing the world, together.

Power to Change the Heart of Man

We need to use the weapons of warfare that God has given us, not the weapons of the world and the weapons of flesh.

> ***Hebrews 4:12*** *For the word of God is living and powerful, and sharper than any two-edged sword, piercing even to the division of soul and spirit, and of joints and marrow, and is a discerner of the thoughts and intents of the heart.*

What cuts asunder, dividing the soul and the spirit, the joints and the marrow? Is it your correction, your opinion, what you think about everyone, and how the Church should change?

Does that divide and cut asunder? Is what you say the discerner of the thoughts and intents of the heart?

Who are we to stand as a god over His Church and tell people what they should think, how they should feel, and how they should do things, when we are not even fulfilling our own function? We, as prophets in office, need to be breaking the hard ground through prayer so that the Holy Spirit may move on the hearts of His people.

THE SPIRIT OF GOD HAS TO BE LOUDER THAN THE SPIRIT OF MAN AND THE SPIRIT OF THE ENEMY.

Last I checked, it is the Word of God that cuts asunder. It is the light that shines forth in the darkness and into our hearts, giving us the revelation of Jesus Christ. It is the Word and the Holy Spirit who bring the cutting of the joints and the marrow and are the discerners of the heart.

We need to give Him that license in His Church, because license has been given to the enemy to counteract what God wants to do. The hearts of God's people have become so cold by hearing the enemy's word again and again.

We have to cut through the noise.

The spirit of God has to be louder than the spirit of man and the spirit of the enemy.

That is only going to happen when we get into our prayer closets and start breaking ground. This will happen when you declare what God has to say into the earth.

We must put our opinions on the shelf and put God's sword in our mouths. Then perhaps, we will cut, change, and have a real impact on the body of Christ. Then, we may start seeing the vision come to pass.

You will learn that when God gives you a vision or a pattern to speak forth, God will begin where you are involved first.

God Will Begin at Home

He will give you the vision for the ministry or church you are involved with first. When He first gives it to you and you start breaking that ground in prayer, the heart that will be called to change first will be your own.

How else will you recognize the readiness of the hearts of everyone else, if you didn't go through the process first?

Here you thought that you have to break this hard ground so that everybody else can see, hear, and know what God wants. Yet, how will you recognize that if you didn't go through the process first?

God will start taking you through the process. He will begin taking you through the hard ground of your heart. Where you started with just a piece of the blueprint or revelation, as you continue to break ground, you will get more and more revelation.

As you get more revelation, not only will it soften your heart, but it will also sow seeds into your heart and that revelation will grow. It is a bit like a prophetic word.

Think of It This Way...

Do you remember the first time that you flowed in prophecy?

You got a little picture or a couple of words. You spoke them out and God gave you another few words, or you spoke the vision and you got another vision. The journey began.

This is the same concept. God gives you a revelation and the first thing that happens is that you hit a hard wall.

Why?

It is because nothing has been built there before.

"Behold, I do a new thing and now it will spring forth. Will you not know it? I will even make roads in the wilderness and rivers in the desert." (Isaiah 43:19)

He will create roads and rivers where there were no roads and rivers before. That means that we have to prepare the ground.

It is so hard when God gives you a new vision because you have not done it before. You are standing in the middle of a wilderness and you have to break the ground. You are standing in the middle of the desert and you need to make a way for water.

It has never been done before, so of course the ground is hard. Did you think that God would give you a vision and it would just come out of heaven ready-made?

Prophet and Apostle – Powerhouse Team!

If so, then you are in the wrong fivefold office. Sorry, you are a prophet. You do not get to have the full picture like the apostle does. He is the one who has to oversee the complete building, but you have to get it down from heaven first.

That is why the two of you work so well together. Now, as you take a piece of that vision and start breaking the ground, that vision will begin to become clearer and clearer. You may just see the first step or a pin scratching of the blueprint.

However, as you continue with this kind of prayer, every time you go to pray you will get an add-on to that vision. You will begin to feel, smell, see, and understand what you are breaking ground for.

Yet, I will warn you. When you start out, all you are going to see is wilderness. All you are going to feel between your toes is very hot, desert sand. You will know that a river needs to run there and that is where most people stop.

You go into prayer for the vision, and you feel nothing. You just feel a wall there, so you stop right there.

After you are done reading this chapter, you will never do that again. In fact, you will realize that you are on the right track. There are many in this world who pack up and go home when they hit their first wall. I am not of that breed and neither are you.

You need to understand – a wall in my path is an invitation to push harder. A battlefield is my inspiration to fight harder. Pressure situations and bad news? That is my trigger to "faith up." When you begin approaching these "spiritual walls" in your prayer life with this kind of attitude, you will soon make your way to the other side.

The Process

The vision comes, and the revelation flows. Then, as the revelation starts to grow, you will get the full picture. Your heart becomes ready for the seed and then their hearts become ready as well.

A momentum begins to build. You will feel it like a shift in the spirit in the congregation. As you continue to break ground, things will start to happen. People will start to pray and cry out to God and hearts will soften.

People who had hard walls will suddenly experience a breaking. Cold hearts will warm up and God will start adjusting the way they think. You will begin to feel that momentum in the spirit together.

Everybody will start feeling an anticipation in the spirit that something is coming. When this happens, your work really begins. Now we enter into the most important part of breaking ground – the preparation of circumstances.

3
BREAKING GROUND: PREPARING CIRCUMSTANCES

In a perfect Church, the best-case scenario would be to have the full fivefold ministry involved in this kind of groundbreaking because it would speed things up. Understand that as I share this concept of "breaking ground" with you that the prophet is not the only one of the fivefold meant to perform this task. The difference lies in how you perform it.

The Fivefold Ministry at Work

For example, the evangelist breaks ground by bringing fire and calling the Church to repentance. The teacher breaks ground with the sword, smashing mindsets, and wrong doctrine. The pastor takes the Church through the process by starting at home with their daily living. He gets his hands dirty!

Of course, the apostle would already have given them a direction, and you, as the prophet, are to speak that process forth and release it into the hearts of God's people through the gifts of the spirit.

God is positioning evangelists and teachers. Why is He doing this?

It is because you have been praying and prophesying, prophet! You have been releasing it over that Church for years!

You thought that you were the one who needed to stand up front, but you do not know what God's people need. Sometimes they need a teacher, sometimes an evangelist, and sometimes just a pastor who can love and bring that change in their hearts.

Getting the hearts of God's people ready is a great starting point. Once they are ready, we need the correct circumstances to make things happen practically.

Think of It This Way...

You need the finances in line, and you need people in the right place at the right time. You need doors to open in this natural world that are shut right now.

You feel the buzz in the spirit. You feel the excitement and anticipation of what God wants to do. You feel it amongst yourselves and you are all excited. Yet, nothing is happening.

Why is it that nothing is happening?

It is because the circumstances are not in line.

This is where the groundbreaking that you do really makes an impact.

***Acts 10:2** A devout man and one who feared God with all his household, who gave alms generously to the people, **and prayed to God always**.*

This scripture is speaking of Cornelius. He was the first Gentile who got saved after Peter received the vision of unclean animals coming down on a tablecloth from the sky. Go and read it.

Pray Always

I want you to really pay attention to those last few words in the scripture above. He did not pray to God once, twice, or three times. He prayed to God... always.

What happened when Cornelius prayed to God always?

It moved the rock, Peter, the apostle, from one place to another. It moved him to a rooftop, to get a message just for Cornelius. It moved an angel to visit Cornelius and give him a visitation.

It moved the voice of God to speak to Peter and to send Peter to Cornelius. Cornelius brought the circumstances in line perfectly so that Peter was in the right place at the right time and available to give that message.

However, Cornelius did not just pray once or twice. He prayed always, and because of that, God looked around and said, "Who can I move? What can I move? What can I arrange to bring this plan to pass?"

Cornelius' heart was always in the right place because it said that he always gave alms, served the Lord, and did what was best. So, his heart was ready, but the circumstances needed to come in line.

He could have sat there with his heart ready, and then died with his heart ready for the gospel. However, until the circumstances came in line for Peter to actually preach the gospel to him, he would have died unsaved.

Our hearts can be ready all we like, but the circumstances need to come in line. The bad thing is that a lot of prophets stop praying when the hearts of God's people are ready.

You hit the first wall and you give up because it has been four days.

Don't forget Moses. He was in the wilderness for 40 years. Beat that!

> DON'T FORGET MOSES. HE WAS IN THE WILDERNESS FOR 40 YEARS. BEAT THAT!

Once you have been praying for 40 years for the same vision, then we can talk about a spiritual blockage. You are a prophet in office and I really hope that you have a bit more authority than that. You should not have to pray for 40 years.

You think you have it bad? After seeing how it was for Moses, I feel good after praying for just four years. How about you? How long has it taken you to pray things through? Do you even have the stickability?

Setting Dominoes in Place

The circumstances need to come in line in order for the vision to be fulfilled. You are basically praying through a set-up of dominoes. When the first one is tipped, the following circumstances have a trigger effect and bring God's plan to pass in this earth.

Imagine, if you will, as you are breaking ground in the hearts of God's people, you are also setting up those dominoes (circumstances). When God takes that first step, it triggers a chain of events that brings His plan to pass fully.

We have not only misunderstood the power of prayer, but also the kind of prayer - especially prophetic prayer. For most believers, we are brought up praying, "Lord, help me pay the bills."

"Lord, please heal me."

I am going so far beyond that. I am not even talking about just getting revelation. Prophets, I am talking about using the authority that God has already given to you to really make things happen. In your ministry, or in your church - faith is powerful.

However, faith alone, without being put to some kind of action, is dead. The best way that we, as prophets, can put that faith to action is with our mouths.

We are to speak forth the creative power of God into this earth so that He can anoint our words and give us the right words to speak at the right time. Then, that will cause the circumstances to come into line.

4
BREAKING GROUND: PREPARING FOR THE VISION

> ***James 5:16*** *Confess your trespasses to one another, and pray for one another, that you may be healed. The effective, fervent prayer of a righteous man avails much.*

The kind of prayer that I am talking about here is not a once-off prayer.

How many more times are you going to wake up feeling a spirit of heaviness and a brick wall in your face, before you get the memo?

PRAYER IS POWER! COMPLAINING IS CHAOS! THEY BOTH ARE A FORCE. WHICH ONE ARE YOU RELEASING INTO THE EARTH?

It is going to take more than praying just once.

Prayer is power! Complaining is chaos! They both are a force. Which one are you releasing into the earth?

You spend five minutes praying and ten minutes complaining because the prayer did not come to pass. Then, you wonder why nothing is happening. You are using a power - just please do it knowing which power you are using.

You spend more time blabbing about what is wrong, what should change, and complaining with a spirit of pride, bitterness, and arrogance. You only spend five or ten minutes in your prayer closet, actually releasing what God wants you to.

You are undoing everything!

"I wonder why nothing is coming to pass?"

You have your prayer time, walk out and say, "Oh, it is still so heavy."

Of course, it is still heavy. You are breaking ground. We have not even gotten to the building part yet. I have not shared yet how Nehemiah and Ezra come along and actually begin to build the temple or the wall.

You do not even have a piece of wall yet. Do you know why you do not have a piece of wall yet?

It is because there is no broken ground to put the foundation of the wall upon. You want your piece of wall. You want to already begin to build your wall and temple. You want to build, but the ground is not yet prepared.

Let me tell you something. The building is the easy part, if the preparations are done correctly. You need to prepare this ground for the seeds.

Stop complaining and start praying! Prepare for the seeds. Prepare the hearts of God's people. I want to repeat, this is not a once-off prayer time. This is not the kind of prayer that you do once a day.

Keep with me here because in the next chapter I will give you five practical steps to follow. I will tell you how you should be approaching this kind of prayer.

That Pesky Prayer Burden

What I am talking about here is the kind of burden that you feel from the moment you wake up in the morning and throughout the day until you go to bed at night.

It kisses you in the forehead when you go to sleep at night, only to punch you in the face the next morning when you wake up. It is lovely. Yes, the life of a prophet is lovely.

No, it is not just you who experiences this. Welcome to prophetic office. (And here we thought it would be all glory...).

When God puts this kind of burden on you to pray, He does not mess around and neither should you. God has given you the tools for this kind of prayer.

Prophetic Authority

It is fascinating when you go from functioning in prophetic ministry and then step up into the fullness of prophetic office authority. You feel the transition take place. What took you hours to pray through before, takes just a fraction of the time now because you have a greater authority.

It is not like you were not being effective before. You were being effective. It just took you a little longer because you were using this really tiny, old-style rake and a horse drawn plow.

However, in prophetic office, it is like riding high on one of those million-dollar tractors. You just go over the land a few times and it is nicely broken up. It is the same kind of work, but with the kind of authority God has given you, it should take you a fraction of the time.

Either way, you still have to break up the ground. It does not get easier to the point where you don't need to do it. Nope, the ground still needs to be broken, but you can get better at it. You cannot miss this process.

Making Bricks – Putting Jesus on the Throne of Circumstances

When I looked at this concept of breaking ground and preparing for the vision, the Lord spoke to me about Solomon.

> *1 Kings 6:7 And the temple, when it was being built, was built with stone finished at the quarry, so that no hammer or chisel or any iron tool was heard in the temple while it was being built.*

When Solomon built the temple, they prepared all the stones and cut them to spec, in the quarry. Once the stones were ready, they transported them from the quarry to the temple, and they assembled it in the temple.

Breaking Ground: Preparing for the Vision

This way, no chiseling or hammering was heard in the temple. When they ran out of stones, they had to go back to the quarry and cut more.

Us prophets – we want to jump straight to assembling perfectly cut stones at the temple site.

You want to see this vision come to pass already but do you have any stones?

"Lord, I do not know what is happening. I am trying to build, but it is not coming together."

It is hard to build a building without any bricks. That is why you do not see a building. So, we go back to the beginning of breaking ground, because it is here that we prepare the hearts of God's people and prepare for the vision.

When you are praying for circumstances to come into line, you are preparing perfectly cut stones. Once the circumstances are in line, it is a simple matter of putting them on top of each other until the picture comes together.

It is a very quick process, just like the dominoes that I mentioned. You push one, and then they all fall in sequence. However, if you didn't prepare the stones first, then you will have nothing to build with later on.

The effort you are putting in now, is the amount of effort you will reap later. That is why this groundbreaking process makes up the bulk of your prayer life. This is where all the prophets, whether in prophetic ministry or office, should have a little tent erected with their name above it that says, "I live here."

Time to Cut Stone, Prophets!

The more prophets, the merrier. It does not take many to assemble and build. However, it takes a lot more to cut heavy building stone to spec. It takes a lot more prayer to soften a hard heart than it does to release the power for that heart to be ignited.

Everybody wants to skip to the exciting part. However, if you do not prepare ahead of time, you won't see the change in the Church that you have been asking God for.

The decrees that I am getting ready to share about later on, are not going to happen without the ground being broken first. The decrees will cause the building to come together and the first domino to be pushed over.

They will bring the kind of creative power that causes entire circumstances and literal bodies and limbs to shift. These decrees will cause your physical body to be healed and your finances to miraculously be changed. However, those kinds of decrees will not happen until the groundbreaking has been completed.

Check Out That Evangelist!

Let's shift gears a little and talk about the evangelists and revivals. Do you know how much preparation and prayer goes into every single one of those huge meetings?

Do you think a man of God can just stand up there and millions are healed and delivered, just like that? Do you think that he just woke up one day and miracles started happening?

That man was on his face before God praying and praying and praying before his first miracle. Even the people God healed were praying and praying and praying.

Do you know how many teams were on their faces before God praying and praying?

"That was a successful revival. What a great man of God."

He got the decree, the word of power that caused that leg to grow, that cancer to be rooted out, that relationship to come right, and that financial miracle to manifest. Yes, he got that word of release.

However, it was the faithful prayer of the just that availed much. That is what allowed him to stand up and speak that word. When are we going to put ourselves in an uncomfortable position to break hard ground?

You need to be in the stone quarry when the sun is beating down on you and you cannot see the change or feel the anointing. You won't know where the power is. You are in the wilderness and there is no food.

Are We Ready for Rain?

You are in the desert and there is no water. Yet, you continue to carve out the rock, according to the instruction from the Holy Spirit, and pray for the rain to come. Then, when the riverbed has been built, the rain may fall.

It is just like we read earlier in Hosea 10:12, "Break up your fallow ground for it is time to seek the Lord, till He comes and rains righteousness on you."

You want God to rain righteousness on you, but are you a vessel on which He can rain? Is your ministry a vessel on which He can rain? Is your church a vessel on which He can rain?

Did you hear what I just said there?

I just said, "Prophets, we have a lot of work to do."

We are sitting around complaining about how things should be different, but preparation is hard work and is very specific to the prophet. Yes, the evangelist is one that will break the hard ground of the hearts of the unsaved and pray for God to bring in the harvest.

In the same way, this particular kind of prayer is part and parcel of your mandate as a prophet. Are you fulfilling your purpose?

You wonder why God keeps pulling you into these circumstances to do nothing but remain hidden and pray. Don't you realize that you are part of something so much bigger than yourself?

Right now, you are birthing something in the spirit that will be here for the next generation to take hold of and run with.

5
BREAKING GROUND: STEPS 1-5

How to Identify When to Break Ground

How do you know when it is time to break ground?

In the chapters that are to follow, I will speak extensively on spiritual birthing, on decree, and on being positioned in the Throne Room. However, how do you know when it is time to either break up ground, or decree and speak from the Throne Room?

It is very easy. God will reveal a new plan and direction. With every new plan or direction that God gives you, with every new position you are put in, with every new ministry vision, and every new plan for the ministry, your first call will be to the wilderness.

"Behold, I do a new thing."

The Lord is so sneaky. He makes this sound so nice. "I'm going to get a new thing!" As if the Lord is going to buy you a cool new pair of shoes.

"He is going to make roads in the wilderness and rivers in the desert."

"Here comes that promotion, people!"

What the Lord does not tell you is that you are going to find your butt in the wilderness and desert, preparing the ground for some apostle to come and give the decree so that the river can flow.

"Great! That is the new thing?"

Yes, it is. Embrace your reality and roll with it.

Whenever God reveals a new direction, vision, or plan, it is time to prepare hearts and circumstances for that plan.

Take nothing for granted and assume nothing. Start preparing for the rain. If God says the rain is coming, start preparing for the rain. Our hearts need to be ready and our circumstances need to be in line.

> *WHENEVER GOD REVEALS A NEW DIRECTION, VISION, OR PLAN, IT IS TIME TO PREPARE HEARTS AND CIRCUMSTANCES FOR THAT PLAN.*

Another sign that you need to break ground is when you wake up feeling continual spiritual heaviness. The plans are not coming together. You pray and you keep hitting wall after wall.

Praying something through is very hard work. You know that God is calling you to pray. So, you get up and pray and pray but leave prayer as tired as you were when you went into prayer. Then, you get up and pray and pray again, but still nothing.

Then, you do it again.

Hard ground!

It has not yet been 40 days. It has barely been 40 hours and you are already complaining. Keep praying until change comes. Pray until your heart changes, your faith increases, and circumstances start coming in line with the Word of God.

When you keep feeling that wall, when you wake up feeling like that ground is smothering you, and when you go to bed feeling the heaviness, God is saying, "It is time to break ground."

Do not sit there saying, "I hope, when I wake up tomorrow, it will be better."

It won't be better! However, we are so stupid. We go to bed and say, "Maybe tomorrow it will get better. We will take this one step at a time. Let's see what happens tomorrow."

Let me solve the mystery for you. What is going to happen tomorrow, is the same thing that happened today, yesterday, and the day before that. When are you going to get up and realize that you need to do something about it?

It is time to break the hard ground.

Step 1: Pray Without Ceasing

> ***1 Thessalonians 5:16-18*** *Rejoice always,*
> *17 Pray without ceasing,*
> *18 In everything give thanks;* ***for this is the will of God in Christ Jesus for you.***

It is the will of God for you to pray without ceasing. It is not my word or idea, telling you to pray it through. It is not my idea saying that you must keep praying until these things come in line. It is the will of God for you.

This is not my will for you. This is not your pastor's will for you. This is the will of God for you. This is not a once-off prayer. It is praying throughout the day, every time you feel that heaviness. It is a continual prayer.

If you continue in this prayer, the decrees will come. You wake up in the morning with that heaviness and you stand against that heaviness and speak forth the Word of God. Keep going.

Then, you go to work, or get started with whatever you need to do for the day, and you feel that heaviness again. You need to pray again. Every time you feel that heaviness, that discouragement, that sand between your toes, that cold wall in your face, or that hammer and chisel in your hand showing you that you are in the quarry, you need to pray.

These are not hour-long prayers. This is not a once-off, "I am going into my prayer closet to specifically pray." This is a continual praying without ceasing. Whenever you feel the heaviness, you push back.

If it comes at you, you push back. When you feel a wall, you knock out a brick. When you feel another wall, you knock out another brick. Do it again and again. It is a continual praying without ceasing, until you get the breakthrough.

You will feel it come in waves. This is my experience. It comes in waves throughout your day. Some days you even feel like you got the breakthrough and it is lighter, but the next day it is heavy again.

Why is it suddenly heavy?

It is either because the hearts are not ready, or because there is another circumstance that still needs to come into line. So, keep praying.

Step 2: Keep Focused

> ***Philippians 3:13*** *Brethren, I do not count myself to have apprehended; but one thing I do, forgetting those things which are behind and reaching forward to those things which are ahead.*

Yes, yesterday was a bad day. You are struggling, and there are problems. Yes, God gave this vision, and nobody got the memo. Yes, the church is a mess. There are mistakes, and the pastor preached the worst message ever on Sunday.

While you are wallowing and complaining, you are not heading towards the prize of the high call of God in Christ Jesus. Instead, your eyes are focused on what the devil wants them focused on – all the problems.

"It is so hard. This wilderness is so rocky, this desert is so hot, and this quarry is so dry. This chisel is so heavy, and I am so tired."

That is all you are looking at and then you wonder why there are no stones with which to build the temple. You wonder why God is not moving in your ministry, why everyone is bickering, fighting, going in their own direction, and pulling their own way.

WHENEVER YOU ARE PRAYING, KEEP YOUR EYES FOCUSED ON THE GOAL.

Are their hearts prepared and are they ready for the vision? Are the circumstances ready?

Whenever you are praying, keep your eyes focused on the goal.

As you are praying throughout the day, as you feel the burden come upon you, it doesn't take long to take a second and see the vision that God gave you.

Think of It This Way…

What direction has God given you for your ministry at the moment? What goal and vision do you have?

If you cannot see a picture, then you have not even gone to the starting point to get a vision from God. You are not even engaging in persistent prayer yet. (This refers to the book *Persistent Prayer: Angels and Demons at Work*[ii])

You do not even know what you should be praying through because you have not looked in the Word, journaled, or asked God what you should be doing.

It could also be that you do not have an apostle, or that you have not spoken to anyone for them to share with you what the vision is. You are just going off on your own, praying here and there. It is no wonder then that you are not seeing any results.

What is your focus and goal? What has God told you that you are meant to be doing as a ministry? What has He told the church that you are involved in?

If you have an apostle, what has God told your apostle? If you are in a local church, what has God told the leadership of that church and what revelation has He given you?

If you are a prophet, sitting at the back of the church, what picture does Jesus have for that church that you are praying through?

Good! You have a picture. Now, I do not want you to just know it. I want you to see it. See what it will look like once that vision has come to pass.

What part are you playing and what part is everyone else playing. Do you see it?

See That Hem!

If you have not even completed the first step, then you cannot expect to have the full picture. Once you have a vision though, every time you pray or feel the burden and heaviness, close your eyes and see that picture. See it in the same way the woman with the issue of blood did. She focused on just one thing as she pushed through the crowd.

She saw the hem of Jesus' garment. She could not see all of Him. I know that because the Word says that there were so many people and that the crowds were pressing around Him. She would have had to bend down to get to the hem of His garment.

Imagine that it is Independence Day and you are watching the fireworks at one of the biggest and best venues ever. You are all standing shoulder to shoulder and people are shoving you here and there.

Then, the President suddenly walks through the crowd at the celebration, and you are trying to get a look at him.

This is how it was for her. She was looking, but she could not see all of Him. Yet, she saw one thing - the hem of His garment. She crawled and pushed through until she grabbed hold of it.

You do not need the whole picture. What little piece of hem do you see?

When you pray, focus with everything that is in you, on that one little revelation that God has given to you. Pray and pray until you get close enough to hold that hem. As you hold the hem, He will stop, look into your face as you look into His, and you will get the full picture.

Keep focused.

Step 3: Pray in the Spirit and With Understanding

> **Romans 8:26** *Likewise the Spirit also helps in our weaknesses. For we do not know what we should pray for as we ought, but the Spirit Himself makes intercession for us with groanings which cannot be uttered.*

> ***1 Corinthians 14:15*** *What is the conclusion then? I will pray with the spirit, and I will also pray with the understanding. I will sing with the spirit, and I will also sing with the understanding.*

When you are praying this through, pray in tongues and also pray the revelation that you see. You are feeling a prayer burden while you are washing the dishes, while working at your desk or driving in the car.

When you do not know what to pray, just put the vision or picture in your mind that God has given you. Focus on it and start speaking in tongues. As you are speaking in tongues, it is like you are focusing your aim.

This way, your spirit, soul, and body are all in accord and you are doing nothing but what God wants you to do. You are in His realm now and under His control.

As you speak in tongues, you will feel the emotion of the vision, the emotion of pushing through and breaking through.

As that vision evolves and you see more, then you can say, "In the name of Jesus, I call that wall to come down. I call the veil over the eyes of God's people to be removed. I soften that hard heart in Jesus' name."

In all of these, you are focused on the goal. These do not need to be hour-long prayers. Although, I am not saying that they cannot end up that way. Sometimes, when God has you birth something, it can be a longer process. We will discuss that later.

However, the kind of groundbreaking that I am talking about here is about short, sharp breaking ground moments throughout your day. This is not a once-off prayer time where you give the decrees from the heavenly realm.

This is something that you can do very quickly, five minutes at a time. You can do it multiple times throughout the day, as the Holy Spirit leads you and as you feel that heaviness. Break ground repetitively!

The more you do it, the quicker you are going to get a breakthrough. Also, the more people involved in doing this, the quicker you will get a breakthrough. Like I said, we have a lot of work to do.

Step 4: Strengthen Yourself in Faith – Use the Word

> ***Hebrews 4:12*** *For the word of God is living and powerful, and sharper than any two-edged sword, piercing even to the division of soul and spirit, and of joints and marrow, and is a discerner of the thoughts and intents of the heart.*

The next step is to strengthen yourself in faith. This is what the Scriptures said of Abraham. He did not waver in his belief or in the promises of God, but he strengthened himself in faith.

He gave glory to God and was fully convinced that what He said He could do, He would perform. Be strengthened in faith and use the Word of God against the problem. Get into the Word and find some passages that are in line with what God is showing you. Then, meditate on those passages.

What is the vision you are birthing? What is the plan? What is God showing you, and what are you heading towards?

Go and find some scriptures that you can stand on to aim at the problem.

Think of It This Way...

Imagine the Word of God like a sword. In front of you is a big watermelon. The watermelon is your problem. Take that sword and slice up that watermelon.

Got the picture?

The Word of God is a nice, sharp sword. It is powerful. I could hammer the watermelon and kick it around and it would still break, but using a sword is more effective. That is what using the Word in this kind of prayer does.

Now, it's not about picking random scriptures. Rather pick scriptures that you have meditated on. In other words, you need to take scriptures that have become your own and that have shaped your spirit. You have been meditating on them for a long time. You believe and see them.

They have become so part of you that they are an extension of your prayer. When you look at a blockage and you are praying through a vision, you aim that scripture at the problem. You use it like a weapon.

It is just like when you are praying in tongues or speaking to a problem and say, "In the name of Jesus, mountain be removed.

In the name of Jesus, I call that circumstance into line. Thank you, Father, that you are making those connections that need to be made. You come in line right now!

At the name of Jesus, every knee will bow, and every tongue will confess.

Behold, I will do a new thing and now it will spring forth. I will make roads in the wilderness and rivers in the desert. Now, river, come forth!"

I am aiming the Word at the vision, the problem, the hard heart, or whatever it is that God has me praying through. It is powerful and effective. At this stage, you will start feeling life coming to your spirit.

You are not just praying from your head, but from your spirit and with a conviction of the Word. At this stage of your prophetic walk you should have spent extensive time meditating on the Word and quoting it.

If you are reading this book after *The Prophetic Warrior*[iii], revise what you learned concerning visualizing the Word in Chapter 11. I taught you how to build pictures into your spirit based on the Word, and how to use those as weapons against the enemy.

Step 5: Bind the Enemy

> ***James 4:7*** *Therefore submit to God. Resist the devil and he will flee from you.*

Finally, you have arrived at the last step. You need to bind the enemy. Resist the devil and he will indeed flee from you. God has given you this land and promise. If you would only be fully convinced that what He said, He will indeed perform, then it would be counted to you as righteousness.

Everything else is a lie from the pit of hell. You don't have to sit and listen to the devil or wrestle with him. You can continually say, "Get off my land, devil. Get out of my way. You, walls of Jericho, you are coming down."

They did not walk around those walls once. They broke ground until the walls came down. Then, even when the walls came down, they had to pick up their swords, go into the city, and engage in hand-to-hand combat.

They had to kill the inhabitants of that city. We just see the walls coming down. Hallelujah that the walls came down... but now you have to pick up your sword and fight.

"We are starting to see a breakthrough. Everyone is motivated and circumstances are coming into line."

You're Not Done Yet

Good! Now, it is time to pick up your sword and fight. You are not done yet. That vision could come to pass, but you could still lose, because you are just staring at the devil as people manifest because their hearts aren't ready for the change.

Could you imagine seeing the walls of Jericho come down and then pulling out a barbecue and starting a big party?

Just the walls came down, not the entire city. There was still a whole city of bad guys in there.

That is what happens. You pray and pray, start seeing a few circumstances come into line, and things are shifting. And so, you start praising the Lord but do not keep breaking ground.

You don't pick up your sword ready to bind the work of the enemy. He runs right over you and steals the blessing, before you even get to see the temple built.

Now is the time to pick up your sword and do spiritual warfare.

These five steps are something that you can do on a daily basis. Daily, you should be speaking forth words in the spirit and with your understanding. As you feel heaviness, you should be coming against it continually with the Word of God and telling satan to get off your land.

NOW IS THE TIME TO PICK UP YOUR SWORD AND DO SPIRITUAL WARFARE.

"Everywhere that the sole of my foot treads, God has given unto me. Be removed and get lost, you spirit of infirmity."

Whatever it is that God has given you, continue to apply these five steps until you get the breakthrough.

Do Not Forget to Praise!

Lastly, do not forget to praise.

> ***Isaiah 61:3*** *"To console those who mourn in Zion, to give them beauty for ashes, the oil of joy for mourning, the garment of praise for the spirit of heaviness; that they may be called trees of righteousness, the planting of the Lord, that He may be glorified."*

Let me tell you a secret. When the battle is heavy and you feel like you cannot push this wall anymore, the bricks are not falling away from you, but on top of you, it can get discouraging.

When you have prayed and prayed but nothing happened and you wonder if you are wasting your time, you need praise to combat the spirit of heaviness. When you feel discouraged after a time of prayer because you know you did not get the breakthrough yet, the ultimate weapon you can pick up is praise.

"Thank you, Lord, for this circumstance. Thank you for putting me in this place. Thank you for what we do have. Thank you that you are bringing this vision to pass. Thank you for every brick we have to tear down.

Thank you for every hard wall we have to break through."

Begin to praise God. Pick up your guitar or whatever you have (my son Dalton's choice "weapon" is a ukulele. Comical cause he is so big and the ukulele so small... but effective!).

Go and worship. Get empowered again. Get into His presence and get filled up again. Tomorrow is going to be another day to break ground and do spiritual warfare.

If you do not get filled up and encouraged in the Lord, then you will get discouraged and drop your sword in the dirt.

You let the sword go because it got tough. You faced disappointments and setbacks. Yes, you know that you have to pick it up and push through.

That is why you need praise. You need praise to be encouraged again. You need it to remind you of the vision again, because in all of this, sometimes you lose sight of the goal.

You lose sight of why you are breaking ground and pushing through so hard. You forget the promise that He is able to perform. You forget that you have a very special place in the body of Christ.

It is only in His presence that He will remind you of that and show you what you were born to do.

You will feel the anointing and it will wash away all the dirt from the quarry. I can imagine how it must have been to prepare the stones for the temple. Workers must have come home, covered in fine dust from head to toe.

SO, HAVING DONE ALL, PUT ON THE WHOLE ARMOR OF GOD AND STAND KNOWING WHO YOU ARE.

The dust was probably coming out of their nose because they breathed it in the whole day. You sneeze and leave behind a cloud of dust. You are sticky, tired, and sunburned. Then, you get into the presence of the Lord and it is like a waterfall that washes all that away, cools you down, and reminds you of the bigger picture.

So, having done all, put on the whole armor of God and stand knowing who you are. Stand in His presence and be equipped and encouraged, because tomorrow you are going to be called to break ground again.

[ii] Toach, Colette. *Persistent Prayer: Angels and Demons at Work.* San Diego, California: Apostolic Movement International LLC, 2020

[iii] Toach, Colette. *Prophetic Warrior: Weapon Training for the Prophet at Arms.* Prophetic Field Guide Series, Vol. 5. 2nd ed. San Diego, California: Apostolic Movement International LLC, 2016

6
OWNING YOUR PIECE OF THE WALL

When Moses stumbled across his burning bush and made his way to Egypt, there was no doubt that both, people and circumstances were in line. Aaron met him along the way. The elders backed him. Finally! The people were ready. They were keen to get out of there. His job was far from over though.

Once the vision has been conceived in the hearts of God's people it needs to be birthed. And so, God calls upon you once again, prophet, to be the midwife, willing and ready to see the process through. One of my favorite biblical characters to illustrate this principle is Nehemiah.

> ***Nehemiah 1:4-6*** *So it was, when I heard these words, that I sat down and wept, and mourned for many days; I was fasting and praying before the God of heaven.*
> *5 And I said: "I pray, Lord God of heaven, O great and awesome God, You who keep Your covenant and mercy with those who love You and observe Your commandments,*
> *6 please let Your ear be attentive and Your eyes open, that You may hear the prayer of Your servant which I pray before You now, day and night, for the children of Israel Your servants,*

> *and confess the sins of the children of Israel which we have sinned against You. Both my father's house and I have sinned.*

What a beautiful picture of what Nehemiah did to break ground. His heart was full of the vision God intended for His people. He desired to build a wall. Yet, before a single brick was put in place, Nehemiah spent much time fasting and praying.

He lamented! He cried out to God! He moved heaven and earth! He brought about change in the hearts of the people and in his circumstances!

> ***Nehemiah 2:18*** *And I told them of the hand of my God which had been good upon me, and also of the king's words that he had spoken to me.* ***So they said, "Let us rise up and build." Then they set their hands to this good work.***
>
> ***Nehemiah 2:4-6*** *Then the king said to me, "What do you request?" So I prayed to the God of heaven.*
> *5 And I said to the king, "If it pleases the king, and if your servant has found favor in your sight, I ask that you send me to Judah, to the city of my fathers' tombs, that I may rebuild it."*
> *6 Then the king said to me (the queen also sitting beside him), "How long will your journey be? And when will you return?" So it pleased the king to send me; and I set him a time.*

Wow! Talk about a dramatic change of events. Doors opened. The work was given the green light. It would have been naïve of anyone to imagine that Nehemiah's job was done at this point. It was not done at all. He was just getting started. There was a lot that had to be done before they could build!

This is where so many prophets fall down. You spend such a long time breaking ground that when you finally see things happen, you plop yourself on your sofa with a big, "Whew! Glad that is over with!"

Hardly. You just aligned people and circumstances. Now you need to move on to the "building" part. You have the materials. People are in place. God has opened doors and shut a few. The pastor has given the vision, and a go ahead. The people have supported it financially. The land, building, services, and circumstances are all lining up beautifully.

Good! While everyone is having a praise party about the goodness of God and what a miracle it is, you see ahead into the spirit. You see that there is much work to be done.

Nehemiah did not waste any time. He evaluated the wall and set organization in place. Part of that organization was to assign every family and clan to a piece of the wall.

Your Piece of the Wall

Now, when you have your face up against a piece of wall, you cannot see the city. You cannot even see the whole wall. You just see a little bit to the left and a little bit to the right. That is all you see. That was all each clan needed to see, until the wall was built.

It's the same for you. God has a very particular part for you to play in the Church. He has set a sword and trowel in your hand and He is asking you to see this vision through now. He has called you to build, but He is also very particular about what part of the wall is yours to build. Remember... you are not in this alone (even if it feels that way sometimes!)

Unfortunately, you can get so busy trying to understand the whole wall that you forgot that God has your face up against this one piece of it, because this is the piece that you are meant to build.

This is why you cannot see anything else. God does not want you to be distracted by anything else. You keep hitting your face on the same part of the wall.

"Man, when am I going to get through this wall?"

When you build it! Do not be like the foolish prophet in Ezekiel 13:3 of whom it says, "You follow your own spirit and have not seen anything!" They did not see, because they were so busy looking at themselves, that they never got into a position to see what God wanted them to see!

Once you have built the portion of the wall God has given to you, He will continue to move you from piece to piece. Every now and again, He will give you that broad view when you are praying universally. So, where is your piece of the wall?

What place has God put you in right now that you cannot run from?

You tried so hard. You complained to God, to your mentors, and to your pastor.

"I am stuck in the same place."

Yes, you are. That "stuck" feeling is your wall. What revelation has been given to you for your wall? Until you pray it through, you are not going to be released from it. So, get on your wall.

Time to Get "Unstuck"

Your piece of the wall is part and parcel of what you broke ground for! You prayed for the people to be ready. You prayed for the circumstances to come in line. Now they have. Good! Take hold of your piece of the wall now and keep praying it through.

You prayed for a piece of land for ministry expansion. The land was bought, doors were opened. Praises! Now see it through! Cover that land. Cover the vision until it is complete.

Perhaps the Lord gave a vision to start a prophetic school in the church. It took you forever to pray it through! You needed trainers, materials, and the people to be open to the vision. God moved heaven and earth! Things happened. Everyone is ready to get going now. Fantastic! This is the fruit of your broken ground. Now you grab hold of your wall and build!

You have to see it through. Are you praying that the right people sign up? Are you standing on your wall watching so that the enemy does not send distractions?

Say that the Lord wanted to release the gifts of the spirit in the church you attend. In one meeting, revival came! People were slain in the spirit! God renovated that church! Fantastic. Are you keeping watch, prophet? Keep building your wall, because your work has just begun. Are you praying that the revival stays pure?

I consider how many pray for revival and how few watch over it until the full work is birthed. A revival is conceived, yet there are no midwifes to see that baby out of the birth canal until it is able to take its first real breath. They rejoice at the conception and leave at the time of travail. The revival dies and the baby is stillborn.

Sure, for the moment it was exciting. The hard ground was broken, and God moved. However, I wonder how many more stillborn babies we must grieve for in the Church, before we see a move that lasts? When will the work of God remain? It is only when the prophets begin to see the process through.

> *I CONSIDER HOW MANY PRAY FOR REVIVAL AND HOW FEW WATCH OVER IT UNTIL THE FULL WORK IS BIRTHED.*

Where are those who will not only rejoice at the time of conception, as Elizabeth did when John the Baptist leaped in her womb, but who will then also continue to be there to hear his father prophesy his name, and declare the road he would walk?

Who was there to follow the process through until John could say, "May I decrease so that He might increase"? Who was still there when the end of John's journey came?

Will you see the process through, prophet? If so, then it's time to take hold of your piece of the wall.

7
WALL BUILDING 101

God will always come knocking when He needs you to build. He will wake you in the middle of the night to remind you to build your piece of the wall. He will tap you on the shoulder in the middle of your workday.

Truth is though that you do not have to wait for a call from heaven before you build. When I wake up in the morning, I have a bunch of work to do. You cannot just wait for your boss to call you every morning and say, "Are you coming to work today?"

If you do that, you won't keep your job for very long. You have to get yourself out of bed, navigate through the traffic, and get to work. That is what we do, right?

It is the same in ministry. You have a job description. You are a prophet in office. That means that you have a place in the Church, and it is your job to do this. It is not a, "do-I-feel-like-it-today" kind of thing.

There is no, "I am not in a prayer kind of mood. I am in a praise kind of mood. So, I am going to go and praise today."

"Sorry boss, I am not going to do the paperwork today. I am not in a 'paperwork kind of mood'. I am just going to do the rounds. I do not feel like doing the paperwork job, so I will just do the one that I want to do."

Prophetic prayer is part of your job description. Are you fulfilling this task daily? You should be, because it is part of your job as a prophet. Do not be the foolish prophet who is like a fox in a desert, wandering around aimlessly. No, you have purpose. Get your focus back and get to work.

If God has placed you in office, it is a position, not a decision.

You actually have to do this stuff. If you want to call yourself a prophet, then take all the job requirements that come along with that position.

IF GOD HAS PLACED YOU IN OFFICE, IT IS A POSITION, NOT A DECISION.

You should be doing this on a daily basis. Nehemiah built that wall in record time and here you are still stuck with one little piece... for how long? It has been weeks, months, and even years and you still have not built a little square of the wall.

Wouldn't you like to build it a little faster?

Then perhaps you should visit the wall a little more often. Just throwing that out there...

Most days, you do not feel like facing that wall. It feels like you wake up with the wall on top of you. It is tiring, especially if you are having to learn to pray it through.

Clear the Debris Daily

> *Nehemiah 4:10 Then Judah said, "The strength of the laborers is failing, and there is so much rubbish that we are not able to build the wall."*

The worst part is that when you walk away from your piece of wall, the enemy comes and tears down what you built overnight and lays all of his debris on it. If you continue to leave it that way, by the time you finally do come back to your wall, what you built a week, two weeks, or a month ago, is a mess and you have to clean up and start again.

That is why this has to be done at least once a day. So, simply come to your prayer closet or wherever you can find some peace and quiet. For some of my team, that place of "peace and quiet" is the bathroom. We had to implement an office policy.

I said, "Guys, the bathroom is right next to my office. I hear everything. No more intercession on the toilet, ok?"

What ministry has to make that kind of rule?

But hey, no excuses! You can always find a quiet place to build in the spirit!

Find Your "Quiet Spot"

What is *your* quiet spot?

If you have kids, I so understand if your "spot" is the shower or bathroom. I do not judge you! I receive my greatest revelations in the shower!

So, go and find your quiet place and begin with submitting and resisting (James 4:7).

In our ministry, we like to pray in twos. You do not have to do this, but this is something I find motivating. We bring two people together to pray and decree, because it is so much easier when you have somebody else to back up and flow with you.

However, if you are on your own and do not have anyone else to pray with, you can still do this. It is just more fun, if you have someone on the wall with you.

It is like doing a workout. If you have someone else there cheering you on, then it is so much easier. It is the same with prayer. When you do not feel like it one day, someone else is dragging you there.

So, if you can find a prayer buddy, that is fantastic. Find a prayer closet and begin with calming your spirit. Get yourself in the zone.

Unburden Yourself

> *1 Peter 5:6-7 Therefore humble yourselves under the mighty hand of God, that He may exalt you in due time, 7 casting all your care upon Him, for He cares for you.*

I am just going to be real with you here. When I go into my prayer closet, sometimes I am still stressed about the fact that my son has still not made his bed, I have been nagged to death by my daughters, and that nobody has done the jobs I asked them to do on Monday and it is now Friday.

I have all this stuff in my head, and I need to come and be used as a mighty vessel for God. I am just thinking, "I want to hurt someone!" My spirit is terrible!

I am not just going to run into prayer and intercession with all that mess going on in there.

Truth is, I have to calm myself down and come to peace first.

Come now, do not pretend that you don't have days like that. I am just crazy enough to say it and put myself in the line of fire.

So, when the world is attacking you and you want to attack it back... get into your prayer closet, take a deep breath, smile and say, "Hello Jesus. I submit myself to you. I give you the unmade bed. I give you the work that has not been done. I give you all my burdens, thoughts in my mind, worries, frustrations, and irritations."

Cast those cares on the Lord. Besides, it's not like He is terribly surprised by your honest prayer. You are not praying this prayer for the Lord's sake – you are praying it for yours! If you do not put those irritations aside before you start praying, they have a nasty way of working their way into your prayer time and then you end up

YOU NEED TO QUIET ALL THE NOISE AROUND YOU. FIND A PLACE THAT IS QUIET SO THAT YOU CAN LISTEN TO WHAT IS IN YOUR SPIRIT VERSUS ALL THE NOISE ON THE OUTSIDE.

decreeing and releasing some things that were probably a little off.

So, get rid of the frustrations and judgments, and everything that made you mad. I find that speaking in tongues for a while also helps. This helps you to tap into the spirit. Speaking in tongues is one of the easiest ways to tap into the spirit, hear the Holy Spirit, and the still small voice within.

You need to quiet all the noise around you. Find a place that is quiet so that you can listen to what is in your spirit versus all the noise on the outside.

As you do that, revelation will begin to flow.

You will get an impression in your spirit or a scripture may come to mind. You may receive a vision. After you have submitted yourself to the Lord, you will come to peace. You can speak in tongues or even worship for a little while, if you want to.

Worshipping helps me tremendously to cut out all the noise. While I am worshipping, I do not hear anything else, except the melody. However, don't spend so much time there that you do not get to pray.

"I had such a good time in the presence of the Lord."

"What did you do?"

"I just had a good time in the presence of the Lord."

"Did you pray?"

"Yeah, I had a good time in the presence of the Lord."

No, you did not do your job. You got a little sidetracked there. We are not just here to praise and worship. That is an entirely different subject. Right now, we are speaking about specifically bringing heaven to earth through decree and prayer.

WARNING! Watch for Spiritual Blockages

So, what happens if you go to the wall and nothing flows? You have submitted, brought your spirit to peace, and now you are waiting on orders and get... nothing. Something is wrong! It's likely that you have a spiritual blockage.

YOU ARE A PROPHET. GOD WANTS TO REVEAL SOMETHING TO YOU. YOU NEED TO COME TO HIM WITH THAT ASSUMPTION.

I suggest that you look for bitterness or irritation - something where you opened the door to the enemy. Go back to where you did hear the voice of the Lord and felt good, and then look at where you are right now feeling this blockage.

That blockage is not there because God does not want to talk to you, it is there because something is up with your spirit.

You are a prophet. God wants to reveal something to you. You need to come to him with that assumption.

He did not place you in prophetic office to make you deaf. He did not go through all this effort to teach you how to hear His voice just so that He could remain silent.

If you flowed once and now you cannot hear anything at all, you have a spiritual blockage.

It is time for you to find out what that is. It is not normal. God will and does want to speak to you. He does want to give you the revelation. So, deal with your own walls and open doors, if you are experiencing a blockage.

When you start to get that revelation and feel that peace, it feels like a bubbling brook.

Pick up Your Trowel

When you deliberately enter your prayer closet with your piece of the wall weighing heavily on your heart, you are going to pick up a lot! Has there been a lot of conflict around this vision lately?

Has the enemy been sending in agents that are messing with the vision you are praying through? Clear the land. You cannot build when there is so much distraction! The first part of your praying will likely consist of speaking blessing and binding the spirit of strife and confusion.

You might see things like a dark cloud hovering over the vision. Perhaps you will feel unsettled in your spirit. Speak in tongues and speak with your understanding. Tell the mist to lift. Take authority over the strife and conflict.

Pray the Vision Through

> ***Habakkuk 2:2-3*** *Then the Lord answered me and said:*
> *"Write the vision*
> *And make it plain on tablets,*
> *That he may run who reads it.*
> *3 For the vision is yet for an appointed time;*
> *But at the end it will speak, and it will not lie.*
> *Though it tarries, wait for it;*
> *Because it will surely come,*
> *It will not tarry.*

When you stand on your battlefield, armed and at peace, you will receive visions. This is why you had to "tarry a while." You had to wait and get your spirit in line to hear what God has to say.

Be encouraged! You will accomplish the first step quicker the more you pray. It should not be taking hours to get your spirit in line. If you are in office, getting in line with the Lord should take minutes.

So, here you are, ready to pray. The Lord will give you a vision and when He does, it's time to run with it! Yup... time to pray it through.

Pray until the vision changes. Do not stand there and tell everybody what the vision is. You are not there to share revelation. You are there to pray.

I see many prophets falling down right here. You sit in a time of prayer where a whole bunch of prophets spend their time telling everybody what their visions are. Nobody prays the vision through, so nothing really happens.

Everyone just goes away saying, "Wow, everyone really gets great revelation in this group." However, no one picked up that vision and ran with it!

You are not fulfilling your purpose, prophet.

You are going to get a vision while you are praying. Pray it through.

BE ENCOURAGED! YOU WILL ACCOMPLISH THE FIRST STEP QUICKER THE MORE YOU PRAY. IT SHOULD NOT BE TAKING HOURS TO GET YOUR SPIRIT IN LINE. IF YOU ARE IN OFFICE, GETTING IN LINE WITH THE LORD SHOULD TAKE MINUTES.

Let's say, for example, that you start out seeing a road that is covered over with fog and mist. You know that this fog has to go so you start praying.

"In the name of Jesus, I call this road cleared up. I call this mist to be removed and for your light to shine, Lord Jesus. I command every last blockage to be removed."

As I start praying, I see the mist clearing. Once the mist has fully cleared, I might see rocks in the road.

I might see stumbling blocks that satan put in our way to cause us to stumble.

"I remove every last one of those rocks, in Jesus' name, and I call this path clear. I prepare the way, Lord, for the move that you are bringing on this work."

Keep praying the vision through until it evolves.

It may be that as you are praying a vision through, it suddenly switches on you. You will go from seeing a road with mist and rocks, to seeing a waterfall.

KEEP PRAYING THE VISION THROUGH UNTIL IT EVOLVES.

The Holy Spirit is saying that you have prayed that part through enough and that He needs you to pray something else. When God reveals what He wants you to pray as a prophet, He is going to do so in types and shadows.

Remember what you learned in *The Way of Dreams and Visions*[iv]? Remember why you were a strange child who lived in a fantasy world, growing up?

It is because the Lord Jesus was gearing you to understand His nature and character. He will always use pictures based on the Word and often even based on what you understand so that you know what you need to pray through.

Identify When God Switches Gears

Again, as the vision switches, you also need to switch gears. Do not try to cling onto the old vision. Sometimes you may be praying a vision through. Let's take the vision of the mist and stones. You pray and pray, and you see the mist clear, but you do not see the stones removed in the spirit.

You see that they are still there, and you think that you need to pray it through, but suddenly the vision changes. You are like, "No, I really feel that there is something on this road."

Yes, but perhaps God or the people involved need more time. He needs you to switch gears and pray something else for now. So then, you switch to the waterfall.

"Thank you, Father, that you are bringing a refreshing, a whole new experience, an abundance of the Holy Spirit, and a manifestation of your glory and external anointing. I release it right now, in the name of Jesus.

Holy Spirit, I give you license to come in your power and authority, to wash away every bit of debris and dirt. Bring an outpouring of your spirit upon us. Give us eyes to see and ears to hear."

Pray that through until the vision switches. You will feel that anointing rising up and you will pour out your guts. You will see things in the spirit and then suddenly everything will become quiet. You will feel like you have emptied yourself in prayer.

[iv] Toach, Colette. *The Way of Dreams and Visions: Interpreting Your Secret Conversion with God*. 3rd ed. San Diego, California: Apostolic Movement International LLC, 2016

8
ENTERING THE THRONE ROOM

Perhaps you can relate a bit with me here. There is a particular turning point that we all come to during our times of prophetic prayer. It is much like the moment that Elijah came to after he had worked through the earthquake and fire!

> *1 Kings 19:12-13 and after the earthquake a fire, but the Lord was not in the fire; and after the fire a still small voice.*
> *13 So it was, when Elijah heard it, that he wrapped his face in his mantle and went out and stood in the entrance of the cave. Suddenly a voice came to him, and said, "What are you doing here, Elijah?"*

You will recognize this specific moment when you were praying or bulldozing, and then felt a sudden increase of the Lord's presence. You might have felt oppression when you first came to build your wall. You might have felt the anointing and you prayed hard. Then just like that... it became really still in the spirit.

The biggest mistake that you can make in that moment is to sigh with relief and say, "It is finished." You couldn't be further from the truth. When this quiet descends is when things are about to get real.

If you follow Elijah's experience you know that after he wrapped his face in his mantle and went out to the

Lord, he and the Lord got real with one another. From here he received instructions that would change the course of history.

If you run out of your prayer closet when this switch happens, you will miss the point of why you entered in the first place!

> *THIS TURNING POINT IS WHERE PRAYER ENDS AND BIRTHING BEGINS.*

This turning point is where prayer ends, and birthing begins.

Up until this point, all you did was to get rid of all the junk satan had thrown on your wall over the last couple of days. You removed all the blockages, took away the dirt, washed away the sand, and made a nice, clean playing field.

Welcome to the Throne Room

When you feel that lull, prophet, you have finally arrived in the Throne Room.

Do not run out, but tarry a while in the deep silence. If you would just open your eyes in that moment, you would realize that you have just entered the Throne Room of God. Now, it is time to receive His mandate, secrets, and pattern so that you may begin to birth them into the earth.

When I come to that point in my prayer time, I feel like I am standing in heavenly places and looking down. I am seeing the circumstances, the mountains, and the roads. I am seeing the ministries that are out of line, the roads that are going off on a detour and need to be brought straight in line.

I am seeing so beyond the vision that we started with. Remember how I said that at times, your face is so stuck up against that wall, that you see nothing else? Well, when you enter the Throne Room, that all changes.

You are seeing beyond your piece of the wall. You are seeing past the wall and moving on to seeing the temple and outlying city. You are starting to understand your part to play. It is only here that you will see how beautifully your puzzle piece fits into the full picture.

As the Lord entrusts this heavenly perspective to you, you will feel His heart for His bride. You will see beyond your ministry, local church, and vision. Your heart will explode with a much fuller picture and when this happens, it is time to birth God's greater plan into this earth.

You are ready to fulfill one of the greatest privileges we can hope to achieve as prophets: to be the surrogate for our Father, called to carry and birth His vision for His Church into the earth.

9
SPIRITUAL BIRTHING FROM THE THRONE ROOM

> ***Galatians 4:19*** *My little children, for whom I labor in birth again until Christ is formed in you.*

Birth is the natural order of things. If anything is to come to pass in this earth, whether natural or spiritual, it has to be birthed. A baby has to be birthed from a womb.

Consider something as simple as a flower. It has to be birthed from a seed to a sapling.

Even when we get saved, what is it called?

The new birth. You are born again.

As God spoke to me about the subject of spiritual birthing, He said, "Colette, this is the natural order of things. This is what I do to bring things to pass in the earth, whether natural or spiritual."

Jesus was not just dropped on the earth fully grown. He was birthed through the pain of labor. Every prophet, every move of God, was birthed. We read how Daniel travailed and birthed until the angel came with a message.

There is nothing that can be done in this earth, without some form of birthing. Whether it is a baby animal or something as simple as a blade of grass, it needs to go through the birthing process to come to pass.

Birthing and this process of travail is how God does things in this earth. God has a blueprint. At one time or another, you have received a piece of that blueprint, and seen a glimpse of what God wants to do in His Church.

You know there is a new move coming. You can feel it like a trembling under the ground. You know that this mighty Church, this city on a hill is coming forth. You feel the ground shaking under your feet.

Do you know how this is going to manifest?

It is going to manifest through travail, and through birthing it continually.

We say, "God, move! God, move!"

Mary had to give birth to the Son of God. In the same way, don't you understand that you are pregnant with a piece of that puzzle?

Reaching Beyond Prophetic Ministry

Until you travail and birth it into this earth, all you have are empty words. All you have is a word of encouragement and exhortation. Now, I am not knocking those things. The Church needs the exhortation and encouragement.

However, I am going a little beyond prophetic ministry here. This is not a book for those who are just dabbling in a little bit of prophetic ministry. I am talking about something much bigger. I am talking about sending forth the kinds of decrees that change a church.

God has given you a spiritual baby. You have fought with this travail and said, "Why can't God just bring it forth?"

Perhaps as I explain this process and get practical, you will understand what has been going on in your times of intercession.

Feeling What God Feels

This will often happen when you enter into times of prayer and decree that I have already taught on. As you enter the Throne Room you will feel a shift in your emotions. The Lord will use the very thing that has gotten you into more trouble than anything else – your emotions!

In this moment your emotions will not be your emotions anymore. You will feel things that do not line up with your natural circumstances. You will feel tremendous joy, when there is nothing to be happy about, and deep sorrow when there is nothing to cry about.

When this happens, know that you are feeling the heartbeat of God. As you continue in this process, something clicks in your spirit. You feel a travail.

If you are a woman who has had children, or a man who has watched your wife give birth, you know the hard work that is involved.

Giving birth is not exactly like sitting on a hammock in Hawaii.

It is messy, bloody, gritty, and grimy. There are tears, blood, umbilical cords, and placenta everywhere. It is a mess. Yet, there has never been a moment in your life when you were more emotionally moved!

The Heart of the Father

As a father, the first time you held your child in your arms, nothing quite prepared you for what you felt in that moment. This is your baby! Without even trying, you feel a sense of protection.

You think, "Heaven help anyone who dares touch this child."

You knew that you would love your child, but nothing prepared you for that moment.

WHEN YOU ENTER THE THRONE ROOM AND THE LORD WANTS YOU TO BIRTH SOMETHING, HE WILL SHARE HIS HEART WITH YOU.

This is the kind of passion that comes out of you when you begin to travail on behalf of the Father.

If our love as natural parents is so fierce, then tell me what do you think the heart of the Father is like when He looks at His children? Don't you realize that the Father looks down on you and is overcome with a fierce sense of protection?

When the Father sees a butcher come to hurt His sheep, don't you think that He wants to take that butcher and punish him?

If you as a natural dad feel these things, how much more your Heavenly Father?

Well, when you enter the Throne Room and the Lord wants you to birth something, He will share His heart with you. Perhaps even as I am sharing, you can recall this happening. The intensity of the emotion can be overwhelming sometimes.

The Travailing Process

I love what Paul said in Galatians, "My little children". Now, the Galatian church did not consist of little children. These were grown men and women, but he saw them as God saw them. He said, "My little children of whom I travail in birth again, until Christ be formed in you."

This is not a once-off process, it is a continual travail.

We all wish that we could just have one contraction and then pop the baby out. After a couple of hours, you think, "Lord, save me. I am going to die. Give me drugs or some sort of pain relief. Make it go away."

I was so big on having a natural birth with my first daughter. Then those contractions hit, and I was like, "What do you have on the shelf?"

There go all of your great ideas... especially for us big mouths.

"I am going to have a natural birth. I am going to handle it gracefully."

You think so? We will talk again after your first experience.

After you have had a couple of children, you are humbler and a little savvier. You walk into the operating room and say, "Get that epidural prepped now."

It is the same with spiritual birthing. You go through one little travail, one prayer time, one decree, and you think your job is done. When did Paul stop travailing?

He did not stop until Christ was formed in the people. Look around you. How many people do you see Christ formed in? How long do you think it took him?

These were people who came from a heathen background. They did not have a Christian background, like some of us have had. They were pagans. They worshipped idols. I can imagine that Paul engaged in a lot of travail.

> PROPHETS ARE THE ONES THAT CONTINUE TO TRAVAIL UNTIL CHRIST IS FORMED IN GOD'S PEOPLE AND UNTIL GOD'S PLAN IS FULFILLED IN THIS EARTH.

Suddenly, you understand why the process that you have been going through is not just a once-off process.

We are not evangelists. We do not just walk in the external anointing and get people saved, filled with the spirit, and our job is done.

Prophets are the ones who continue to travail until Christ is formed in God's people and until God's plan is fulfilled in this earth.

The Purpose of Spiritual Birthing

What is the purpose of spiritual birthing?

> ***Isaiah 66:8-9*** *Who has heard such a thing? Who has seen such things? Shall the earth be made to give birth in one day? Or shall a nation be born at once? For as soon as Zion was in labor, she gave birth to her children.*
> *9 Shall I bring to the time of birth, and not cause delivery?" says the Lord. "Shall I who cause delivery shut up the womb?" says your God.*

How long have you been in travail for the vision that God has given you for the Church? How long have you struggled with this process? Did you think that He would bring you through travail and not give birth? Did you think He would put you through this process to give birth to a stillborn child?

No, not at all.

Your problem is simply that you keep getting off the birthing table. You are one of those women who get to that transition phase and say, "This is too difficult. I am out of here. Take this away. I am done with this. I am finished with all these contractions and all this pain."

Paying the Price Others Will Not Pay

Tarry a while. Pay the price that the Church will not pay.

Prophets, you are called to pay a price that the Church will not. To whom much is given, much is required. Are you still sure that you want to be the second highest office in the fivefold ministry?

Did you think this was all about pomp and ceremony? Did you really think it was all about honor and glory?

No, it is about paying the price that no one else is willing to pay.

Isn't this so, even in the natural?

You look at a CEO of a business and think, "He can do whatever he wants. He can work whenever he wants and chill whenever he wants."

Do you know the price these people pay? Don't you realize that they have given their lives into their business?

They work harder than anyone else. They carry a load of responsibility and care. They are the ones lying awake at night asking, "Am I going to be able to pay my employees this month?"

An employee doesn't care. They just go to work, do their job, get their salary, and go home. They just need to worry about not getting fired. It is the guy at the top who has to take everybody into account.

Spiritual Birthing From the Throne Room

He has to make sure the team is working efficiently, and the business deals are closed. They carry a load of responsibility, but many only see the money and position. You do not see the load. Anybody who has been there knows what I am talking about.

It is the same for the Church. Some look at prophets thinking, "You have it so easy."

Anyone who is in prophetic office thinks, "Are you psycho? Easy?! You don't know what a prophet is, do you? Those two words, 'prophet' and 'easy', do not belong together!"

YOU ARE CALLED TO STAND NAKED, GO THROUGH THE FIRE, AND EXPERIENCE THE HEART OF GOD AND SO GAIN THE MIND OF CHRIST.

A prophet is called to pay a price that the church is not prepared to pay.

"How come they do not have to go through this process?"

They are not prophets.

"Why only me? Why am I the one who has to pay the price?"

Well, you can just go and be an evangelist, if you like…?! There is nothing wrong with evangelists. They are amazing and do a fantastic job, but they are paying their own price and are not called to pay the price God asked you to pay!

Do not whine at me because you are a prophet and you have to pay a price. What did you expect?

You are called to travail and push through.

You are called to stand naked, go through the fire, and experience the heart of God and so gain the mind of Christ.

Yes, we travail through our walk and experience, going through what others do not go through. We go through the fire that others do not go through. We are stripped and made naked, like others are not.

We get rejected. We go through and travail continually. We are birthing like Mary did, in a stable, doing the work that no one else wants to do. It's a weighty call and not one for wannabes who think they are in it for the fame.

The humbling process we go through to qualify to feel the heart of the Father in this way is best lived, rather than explained.

10
SPIRITUAL BIRTHING: THE TRAVAILING PROCESS

> ***Romans 8:26*** *Likewise the Spirit also helps in our weaknesses. For we do not know what we should pray for as we ought, but the Spirit Himself makes intercession for us with groanings which cannot be uttered.*

I already shared how the birthing process is an occurrence that will take place when you enter the Throne Room. This is not the same as prayer or decree. Rather it is a very specific vision that God will make you "pregnant" with spiritually. In fact, you might find that you will birth like this in seasons.

What makes this so powerful is how the Lord uses your emotions to help you birth the vision.

In fact, when you birth spiritually, Romans 8:26 becomes real to you! Your "time of prayer" simply gets hijacked by the Holy Spirit and He is the one who is now doing the praying. He is making intercession for you and it often comes with groanings that cannot be uttered.

The Birthing Experience

When the Lord begins birthing something through me, I feel like weeping or laughing. For me, it sometimes comes upon me so strongly that I feel it in my body. I feel it as if I am birthing something naturally. My stomach muscles clench up.

The more I pray, I experience what God is experiencing. He is the one birthing His plan into the earth. He is the one bringing it to pass. As prophets, birthing is what gets the ball rolling.

You cannot have a full-grown child before you have a baby.

Until a birth has taken place, there cannot be decree and prophecy.

I could say to my husband, "Let's have another child."

Firstly, he would give me a funny look. Then, he would likely let me have what I want because he is good like that.

Then, I'd say to myself, "We are going to put our son in college. He is going to have a career in law, and he should play baseball."

There is one little problem. I don't actually have him yet. That is what you are doing when you send out all those decrees before birthing. Then, you wonder why nothing is happening.

UNTIL A BIRTH HAS TAKEN PLACE, THERE CANNOT BE DECREE AND PROPHECY.

You prophesy and prophesy, but there is no growth. Did you birth the baby?

You have built a beautiful nursery. You have the child's life all planned out and you have booked him into the best college.

Pity there is no child. How unfortunate!

This is foolish, right? Yet, isn't this what we are doing?

Putting Things Into Order

We sometimes make the mistake of beginning at the end! We jump in with prophecy and decree, trying to work our way to birthing. However, nothing can begin until we have birthed something new.

When you intercede you just want to get in there and stomp on the devil's face, decree, and speak forth. There is nothing wrong with that, but back up a little. Did you birth it first and bring God's plan into this earth?

How are God's promises going to come to pass?

"I just cannot wait until Jesus manifests Himself, right here in front of me."

Mary had to give birth. There has to be a birthing process. This is our starting point to seeing universal change in the Church and earth.

Until you have birthed a focus, what are you praying for?

Your groundbreaking gave you a piece of wall. Spiritual birthing gives you the full picture along with your place in that picture. As a prophet, it allows you to birth the weapons of warfare others need to carry.

YOU WANT TO BUILD, BUT YOU DID NOT BIRTH. YOU WANT TO ESTABLISH, BUT YOU DID NOT TRAVAIL.

As a prophet, spiritual birthing allows you to release the blueprints in the spirit for the apostles to receive and build the temple with. It allows you to position the fivefold ministry where they can be most effective.

You want to build, but you did not birth. You want to establish, but you did not travail.

Think of It This Way...

When it comes to spiritual birthing, you cannot make it up. You can make up a prophetic word though. Trust me, I have seen it done. However, you cannot make up a spiritual birthing experience.

> *1 Corinthians 13:12 For now we see in a mirror, dimly, but then face to face. Now I know in part, but then I shall know just as I also am known.*

I am taking you deeper. I am taking you beyond the gifts of the spirit and prophesying over people. These practices break ground. These aspects of your ministry bring you into the Throne Room. However, I am talking about a birthing experience. When you are birthing, you feel the heart of God. You know as you are known. Where before you just knew in part, you now know face-to-face.

Excuse me if I seem to be repeating myself. I just cannot emphasize enough the fullness of what it means to feel as God feels.

After such an experience, you know what God wants to do in this earth. How many prophets say, "Well, I think this is the Lord? I sense this is the direction that He wants to take us in. I got this great revelation that this is what God wants to do."

When you birth something in the spirit, trust me, you know. You ladies who have had a natural birthing experience, did not give birth and say, "Oops! What happened there? Where did you come from?"

Don't you wish?

"Whoopsie daisy... there it is."

No! When you have birthed and travailed, nearly breaking your husband's hand, swearing at him repeatedly - you know this child is his!

It is the same with spiritual birthing. When you feel the heartbeat of God and He gives you the revelation, you feel it. You are surrounded by it. There is no denying who the Father is!

Birthing for Others

As a prophet, you are not always going to birth for yourself. In fact, I would daresay that most of the birthing is going to be done for others.

This is because our minds get clouded sometimes. And so, we don't pick up God's heart because our own emotions are too strong. It is a whole lot easier to be objective about someone else's ministry.

Where does God have you right now? Are you serving in someone else's ministry? Are you a prophet in office for the Church universal and God has been putting His plan and pattern for His Church on your heart?

My Personal Experience

That is certainly where my birthing experiences take place. You will be in prayer and you will receive visions and impressions.

For me, the mighty warriors were often one of the things that God had me travail for continually. It was always the same vision. This was right at the beginning when we started our first prophetic school in 1999.

I began having these experiences and God kept showing me His mighty warriors. He said, "My gladiators, my mighty warriors, are out there in the world. However, they are hidden like seeds in the soil. Colette, you need to call them out."

I would pray and see seeds in the ground. Then, I would feel a burden in the spirit and a heaviness would come on me. Sometimes, I did not even know the words I was praying. I would just pray in tongues or weep.

I would groan before the Lord, weeping, "Father, your people. Father, your people."

> ***Daniel 9:3*** *Then I set my face toward the Lord God to make request by prayer and supplications, with fasting, sackcloth, and ashes.*

I can imagine that this must have been what it was like for Daniel when he was praying on behalf of his nation. He was travailing and had a deep experience.

"Father, you promised. Now is the time for your promise. Father, your people."

You pray it through and pray it through. I could go for an hour or two, just travailing and crying before the Lord. Then, I would suddenly feel the burden lift. When I went back to pray later about something else, He would take me back to that again and again.

That was over 20 years ago and here you are, reading my book. Over 20 years ago, I was in the backside of the desert, on my face before God, praying for you to rise up!

Through the years, I have seen God raise His mighty warriors up and I cannot begin to tell you how many I have come across in the middle of nowhere.

God would send us to the most obscure places and have us pick up just one person in the middle of nowhere - in a town that you have never heard of. These are mighty warriors. Our ministry is now completely built with them.

Birthing the Fivefold

Long before we even went public with our ministry, Craig and I travailed tirelessly in our prayer closets. We did not even know what part we would play in the new move that was to come. We just knew that a new move was coming where God was raising up the fivefold ministry.

I knew as I prayed, they were going through training in the wilderness, and in the world. I often saw them going through hard times, in the fire, confused, and unsure of their call. Satan was buffeting them to the left and right.

I would travail.

"Father, pluck them out of the fire. Bring them out of the wilderness, Lord. Put them where you need to put them."

I doubt very much that I was alone in my travail. Do you know how many prophets have been travailing like this for years?

The Fruit of Today From Yesterday's Travail

Is it any surprise that we see apostles and prophets popping up everywhere we look? The prophets birthed the move on which we are now riding. Everybody wants to jump on a surfboard and ride the crest of the wave.

Yet, it was the true men and women of God, who were on their face groaning and travailing before God, who birthed what we are seeing today.

It is time to birth again, prophet. There is much more that God is doing. We need to birth this apostolic move. We need to be as Nehemiah and build the walls to protect it. We need to call out God's true apostles to take over in all of the systems.

This way, this world can be for our Lord. We need leaders who are not afraid to rock the boat, to be bold, to be politically incorrect and say it like it is.

> *WE NEED CHANGE, SO WE NEED MEN AND WOMEN WHO ARE PREPARED TO BRING THAT CHANGE.*

We need change, so we need men and women who are prepared to bring that change.

That is God's plan and pattern. That is what He wants. You are praying and praying, but are you birthing?

11
SPIRITUAL BIRTHING: THE STEPS OF THE TRAVAILING PROCESS

When God wants to do something in this earth, He uses man. He gave Adam authority over this earth at the very beginning. That authority has been passed down to us.

When God wants a pattern to come to pass, He comes knocking on someone's door.

He went to Noah and said, "Build me a boat."

GOD HAS THIS PATTERN AND PLAN THAT HE WANTS TO IMPLEMENT IN THIS EARTH BUT HE NEEDS SOMEONE TO RELEASE IT.

He put a prayer burden on Daniel. He visited Gideon. He called out to Samuel. Every time God wanted to do something magnificent, He came knocking and looking for a vessel.

How much more in the New Testament where we have the Holy Spirit dwelling within us?

God has this pattern and plan that he wants to implement in this earth but he needs someone to release it.

His will is released through words and actions. How powerful is it that we can pray, receive, and conceive the pattern of God and go through a labor process as God would go through a labor process?

Together, He and us, birth His plans in this earth. That is quite a responsibility.

God Working With Man

As you are travailing and releasing these kinds of prayers, you are releasing a force.

When you birth like this in the spirit, your mind, emotions, will, spirit, and body are all completely His. You feel what He feels and want what He wants. You think what He thinks, and you speak accordingly.

The power that comes as a result can uproot mountains. It can tear down and build up.

Something always happens when I birth like this. It is not because I am such a great prophet though. It is because He is such a great God. He just needed a vessel. His power does the work, but His power needs an outlet.

JESUS NEEDS SOMEBODY TO SPEAK HIS WORD AND ACT OUT HIS ACTIONS, BECAUSE THE THINGS THAT ARE RELEASED IN HEAVEN, NEED TO BE RELEASED IN EARTH.

Jesus needs somebody to speak His word and act out His actions, because the things that are released in heaven, need to be released in earth.

> ***Matthew 18:18*** *"Assuredly, I say to you, whatever you bind on earth will be bound in heaven, and whatever you loose on earth will be loosed in heaven.*

When Spiritual Birthing Takes Place

There are very specific times when these birthing times occur.

However, I cannot go in and plan to birth. I am just required to be in the spirit, put my cares aside, and be available to the Lord. It will come upon you when the Father says that the baby is ready! Just like in the natural! Some babies come on time. Some come early. Some are overdue and no matter when you want this to happen, the baby decides! You are not in control.

When you make yourself available, it will happen. That is why praise and worship are some of the best ways to prepare yourself.

This gets your mind out of the way and your emotions in line with God's. If you can feel God's emotion, you are halfway there. If there is anything to birth, and you are in touch with His emotions, you will feel the travail that God is going through to birth this thing in the earth. (Revisit *Prophetic Anointing*[v] for more on that principle.)

> ***John 11:35-38*** *Jesus wept.*
> *36 Then the Jews said, "See how He loved him!"*
> *37 And some of them said, "Could not this Man, who opened the eyes of the blind, also have kept*

> *this man from dying?"*
> *38 Then Jesus, again groaning in Himself, came to the tomb. It was a cave, and a stone lay against it.*

What happened after Jesus wept before that tomb?

The dead was brought back to life and God's plan was made manifest in the earth.

What happens after you travail?

What Spiritual Birthing Looks Like

So, now that you have the concept in place, let's take a practical look at what spiritual birthing is like in real time!

1. Intense Emotions

The first thing that will happen when God wants to use you in this way, is that you will feel an onset of emotions you might not be able to explain.

You may be in your prayer closet, or you may even just be going about your business. The Lord will begin to draw you to Himself. He will call you out. Even if you are not in your prayer closet you might find that you keep getting "distracted" with the things of the Lord. You feel the drawing to be with Him. He won't just jump on you and have you birth in the middle of the street.

The first time this happens you might feel confused. You might feel like weeping for no reason. You might feel anxious or overly full of joy.

You think, "What was that? What is wrong?"

Go and find a quiet place and weep and struggle with what you are feeling inside.

2. Feeling It Physically

At times, you may feel it physically because your body will be affected by the Holy Spirit. You are feeling physically what the Lord is feeling. Isn't that what the anointing does?

If you have been in a revival or an evangelistic meeting, you know that when the anointing is present you can feel it tangibly.

Of course, you feel it physically! When God moves on man, you feel it. You feel His heart.

What I call the "gentle breeze of Jesus" is more of an internal, inner healing anointing. It is really sweet, and it feels like a nice breeze on a hot day. You may also feel it like oil being poured over you, or like the feeling of being warm and wrapped up.

That is the effect of the anointing, right?

Whenever God moves on man, you feel it. How much more in spiritual birthing? The feeling that you will have in your natural body will be a lot more intense. Your stomach muscles may even clench.

I remember Nate experiencing this for the first time. When I impart to my spiritual children, they pick up everything that I have. Things start happening to them and they come back saying, "What is wrong with me?"

He came to me and said, "Mom, there is something wrong in me. I go to prayer and I just suddenly start weeping and then I get this knot in my stomach."

He thought at first that the enemy was trying to interfere with what God wanted, so he kept binding it, not realizing it was a call to spiritual birthing!

I know it sounds funny, but when you do not know what is going on you tend to think you are a little crazy.

Some Boundaries

NOTE: This experience is not for the pulpit. This is not pretty.

How many prophets are trying to do this behind the pulpit? I am so embarrassed for them when they do that.

HOW MANY PROPHETS ARE TRYING TO DO THIS BEHIND THE PULPIT? I AM SO EMBARRASSED FOR THEM WHEN THEY DO THAT.

I am thinking, "I do not need to see all that amniotic fluid running all over the place? Get back inside!" This is not a show, this is a powerful purpose that God has given to us as prophets.

As in the natural, a woman gives birth with her husband at her side, so is it with you and the Holy Spirit. This is a private affair.

Consider the Old and New Testament prophets who went through their times of birthing. When this process was completed, only then did they step out to decree and prophesy. Daniel travailed alone for Israel. Jacob wrestled with the angel alone until dawn.

This process is not pretty and completely inappropriate to do in front of crowds. Our objective here is to bring results – not to try to prove our prophetic office.

You are going to feel, weep, laugh, be angry, and speak in tongues. Sometimes you will not have words to utter because of the intensity of what you are feeling.

I recommend speaking in tongues because at that stage you do not even know what the baby looks like. Even in the natural, until you give birth, you don't know what the baby looks like.

3. Tears and Loss of Words

> ***Romans 8:26*** *Likewise the Spirit also helps in our weaknesses. For we do not know what we should pray for as we ought, but the Spirit Himself makes intercession for us[b] with groanings which cannot be uttered.*

We already covered this passage. It's for this reason that I recommend that you let the Holy Spirit pray. It is so much easier than trying to understand everything that is going on with your mind.

You are now the Lord's vessel. He has taken charge of your spirit, soul, and body. It is an incredible experience. You begin groaning, speaking in tongues, and travailing. You'll feel tears and you won't know what to say.

You may just groan for a while and then go back to tongues. Then, perhaps a word or two will come out. Perhaps you will see a vision, speak the vision forth, and then go back to travailing. Keep going until the baby is born.

4. The Baby Is Born

When the baby is born, you will feel a sudden release. You will feel like you have just been emptied and you will be physically tired.

We were having a good discussion about the difference between how an evangelist and a prophet flow.

For an evangelist, the Holy Spirit comes upon them from without. They stand as God leads and releases His power over people. They can probably minister a lot longer than a prophet can. I love evangelists for their boldness, but a lot of the time they are not so caught in their emotions as we are when we do God's work.

The evangelist acts out on what they *know* God wants. The prophet acts out of what they *feel* God wants.

Why is this?

It is because a prophet flows from within. You empty yourself when you minister.

Your emotions and God's emotions, your thoughts and God's thoughts, are all wrapped up together.

You are giving all you got for this thing. Your heart and soul are fully engaged. As you travail, you will come to a point when you feel a release. The words and groaning will stop.

Sometimes this is immediate, and other times it tapers off. In that moment, you will feel weary and you will know that you accomplished what you needed to. You just birthed something new into the earth. Then, when you come back to your prayer closet after that season, and continue to pray, the decrees will come.

You will get visions and words of decree. That is the time to come to the Lord and speak forth what He gives you. That is why visions are probably one of the most powerful ways to approach this.

> *YOUR EMOTIONS AND GOD'S EMOTIONS, YOUR THOUGHTS AND GOD'S THOUGHTS, ARE ALL WRAPPED UP TOGETHER.*

I also recommend when you come back to your prayer closet after you have gone through a birthing experience, to bring that experience to mind again.

Keep This Focus

How do you follow up a birthing experience? We will go more into that shortly, but after you have birthed something in the spirit, you will come back and find decrees waiting to be spoken!

In fact, you will get the decrees according to that particular focus. Please remember this! God will give you revelation according to what you focus on. He will steer your focus, but He will only give you revelation according to what you pray.

5. Decree and Warfare

Then, it will be time to step out and continue on that prayer wall to build. Afterwards, God will open the doors for you to decree. This is when you will practically work with people to bring that to pass.

Now is when the doors will open, the ministry opportunities will come, and the contacts will be made. Suddenly, out of nowhere, those doors will be open.

After this when you come back to pray, it is time for decree or spiritual warfare. Either another door needs to be opened or you need to protect this newborn.

More often than not decree after decree will be waiting for you. There is a lot of building to do now, prophet! I have dedicated a couple of chapters to decree and prophecy, so I am not going to say terribly much about that here.

However, I do want to bring to your attention how exciting this part is! When you begin to decree after birthing in the spirit, your faith will ride high!

Do you know without a doubt that the words of decree will not return void? You can have that confidence if you birthed first! So, you could keep running around and telling random strangers, "I declare and decree... " or, you could become available to birth in the spirit and then send out atom bombs of decree that hit their mark every time.

6. Prophecy – Keeping the Midwives Motivated

Once you have begun to build, then it is time for you to work with people. It is for you to teach and motivate them.

There is something about having gone through the process that gives you a confidence and boldness to step out there and say what you need to say. It is because it became your reality a long time ago.

You do not have any fear to say what you need to say because you have been living this reality in the spirit for some time. You know that you know that you have heard from God. You are not thinking, "I hope I heard from the Lord." How often do we try so hard to stand in faith, praying that God will come through for us?

Well, did you go through the process? You are not even sure of your conception and you want to have a baby shower? No, once you have allowed the Holy Spirit to birth through you, you do not need to "drum up" faith. You have it, because you have travailed long for it.

There is no uncertainty any longer. There is no doubt in your mind that this promise is coming to pass. You have been living and breathing it day after day.

This subject of decree and prophecy have their own chapters, so I am going to cut this short now and touch briefly on every prophet's favorite subject… spiritual warfare!

---

[v] Toach, Colette. *Prophetic Anointing: Anointed to Worship.* Prophetic Field Guide Series, Vol. 3. 2nd ed. San Diego, California: Apostolic Movement International LLC, 2016

12
SPIRITUAL WARFARE FROM THE THRONE ROOM

Now things are getting good! Fired up and ready to go? Good, because now it is time for action. Time to pick up your sword and fight the hordes of hell!

> ***Ephesians 6:10-11*** *Finally, my brethren, be strong in the Lord and in the power of His might. 11 Put on the whole armor of God, that you may be able to stand against the wiles of the devil.*

I love how Apostle Paul starts this passage. He starts it with, "Finally!" Yes! Finally, it is time. Finally, after you have done all else, it is time to stand in the authority God has given to you.

So, you transition into the Throne Room. This time you are not called to birth anything. Remember, spiritual birthing comes in seasons. It will not happen every single time you enter the Throne Room.

What can happen though is that the Lord will call you instead to protect this baby you birthed! When you are called to warfare things get sweet and quiet. You realize it's time to press in. You press in.

You feel His presence but at the same time feel like you hit a wall. You might doubt yourself. You might think,

"Hmmm, maybe I am pushing too hard here. Maybe the Lord just wants me to be silent."

Nope, you are hitting the resistance that the enemy put in your face. Now, the amount of groundbreaking you have been doing, will determine how easy or difficult your warfare will be. As an apostle, if the prophets have been doing a lot of groundbreaking, when I get to this stage, the heavens open up!

Revelations flow. I see the demonic bondage that is restricting the work of God. I might see either the demons at work or the plans that the enemy has put in motion in this earth. Now, if the groundwork has not been done, you are in for a bit of a grind. It will mean picking up your sword and continuing to stand in faith against the work of the enemy.

That is why I started you off with a lesson on breaking ground. That was preparing you for what was to come as you got down to the nitty-gritty of it! If that groundbreaking has not been done, you will enter the Throne Room wanting to decree and sow seeds, but the ground will be as hard as can be.

Keeping Your Baby Safe

> ***Revelation 12:4*** *His tail drew a third of the stars of heaven and threw them to the earth. And the dragon stood before the woman who was ready to give birth, to devour her Child as soon as it was born.*

This scripture aptly describes the kind of warfare you will engage in when you have completed the spiritual birthing process. The enemy waits to consume what you have done in the spirit.

Recognize that we do not wrestle with flesh and blood! God will open the door and the enemy will put obstacles in the way. Just as in the natural an enemy will counter-attack, do not be surprised if after you have released God's word that you get a counter-attack as well!

This is not a time to be discouraged. The doors have opened. You have seen God move. Things are starting to look up. Out of nowhere you take a hit. Pick up your sword, prophet. It is time to protect the baby that God has had you release! This is not a time to sit back and relax. Rather, it is time to stand guard and protect this to the very end.

Just as a baby is vulnerable to the elements in the natural, so also is this spiritual baby vulnerable. When I pray something like this through, I see either a baby or a little seed that has sprouted into a sapling. The winds and rains come to try and wash it away. The sun bakes down on it.

Day after day of doing warfare and speaking protection, I see that sapling becoming strong until it is a tree that can withstand the elements. So, guard jealously over the babies you have birthed in the spirit. See it through.

The Enemy Will Be Revealed

As you stand guard over this spiritual baby, you are going to see the rulers, powers, and princes that are coming against the Lord's plan. Sometimes it takes a bit of time to uncover him. The nature of the enemy is to hide his face. He hides behind actions made by man. When you take your eyes off offense and turn them to the offender, you get fresh insight.

It is here that you will stand against Pharaoh with regards to the financial system, and the Prince of Tyre with regards to the marketplace. You will see all the systems of the world that have been choking the life out of the ministry and the Church.

You will come face-to-face with them. This is the time to take what God has given you to take them down and put Jesus on the throne. Remember what you learned in the chapter on "Displacement Warfare" in the *Strategies of War*[vi] book?

Build up, Tear Down

So, you see the prince of the air that is behind the attack. Time to take your warfare even further.

It's really not good enough to just see demons. As a prophet, you are called to undo their work!

Think of It This Way...

The enemy has been given license in the earth. He has used that license to fulfill his plan, and to counteract what God intends.

To fulfill his purpose, he will use this world and these natural systems, to do his bidding. He will infiltrate. He will use what is available to him!

IT'S REALLY NOT GOOD ENOUGH TO JUST SEE DEMONS. AS A PROPHET, YOU ARE CALLED TO UNDO THEIR WORK!

Think about how the Holy Spirit fulfills His purpose in this earth. He uses the elements of this natural world to bring about His purpose. The natural walls of Jericho came down after the Israelites circled them. I watched a fascinating documentary regarding Jericho. As it turns out, this city was built on a fault line.

So, when the priests blew their trumpets and the people shouted, the Lord set off an earthquake and took that city down! The fault line was always there. The Lord used what was right there to bring about His perfect plan. All He needed was for man to play his part.

The enemy is a copycat, imitating what the Father does. He too will use what is at his disposal in this earth. So, prophet, when you come to pray, you need to go beyond just binding the enemy. You need to counteract his plan in this earth!

You need to displace satan's work with God's plan. This is when you tear down the kingdom of darkness and give God license in the earth.

This can be a very large part of your prayer time, depending on the kind of building and tearing down that God wants you to do.

Remember, that is what He told the prophet Jeremiah.

"I called you to build up and to tear down."

So, this means calling systems into line. It means praying and dethroning the powers in this world, so that the Church can benefit. It means calling the financial systems into line with God's will so that the ministry you are praying for, will be blessed.

Tear down the work of the enemy. Build up the work of God! I take this subject to a much deeper level in *Strategies of War*[vii] about how you can continue this kind of warfare in the natural. So, pick up that book for more on this. I do not want to repeat myself here, but rather want to get on to, in my opinion, the most empowering part of your prayer - decree and release!

> YOU NEED TO DISPLACE SATAN'S WORK WITH GOD'S PLAN. THIS IS WHEN YOU TEAR DOWN THE KINGDOM OF DARKNESS AND GIVE GOD LICENSE IN THE EARTH.

[vi] Toach, Colette. *Strategies of War: Battle Plans for the Modern Day Christian.* 2nd ed. San Diego, California: Apostolic Movement International LLC, 2017

[vii] Toach, Colette. *Strategies of War: Battle Plans for the Modern Day Christian.* 2nd ed. San Diego, California: Apostolic Movement International LLC, 2017

13
DECREE AND PROPHECY FROM THE THRONE ROOM

Put your trumpet to your lips, prophet! It's time to bring the hand of God down so hard that you cause an earthquake to shake this world!

It is truly, only when the words of God are released into this earth, that true change begins. You have cleared the ground. You have birthed God's plan. You have removed the hindrances from the enemy.

Now, step back, world, because the Father is about to take center stage and speak His mind!

You Are Positioned

> ***1 Samuel 3:19*** *So Samuel grew, and the Lord was with him and let none of his words fall to the ground.*

You are finally positioned, prophet. Everybody talks about positioning. There are only two positions that the prophet in office should fully understand and possess continually. The first and most important position is on the cross.

The second one is before the Father in the Throne Room, releasing His word into the earth. That is what it means to be positioned.

You have been waiting to be positioned. However, are you prepared to go through, pray the vision through, and to push through the warfare, until you are positioned in the Throne Room with the anointing and power to speak that pattern forth?

Change Your Approach

Many make the mistake of thinking that just because they received an impression or saw a vision, that they are releasing a decree. This is not so. I remember a particular ministry tour I did with my team through South Africa and Europe. The theme was how to enter into praise and worship. After a few meetings, I had to sit everyone down and have a talk.

WHEN YOU SPEAK ON BEHALF OF GOD INSTEAD OF INTERPRETING FOR GOD, THE POWER COMES DOWN. WATCH FOR THAT EARTHQUAKE!

I had to say, "Ok guys, people did not come here to hear what you or I have to say. They did not come here to hear, 'I sense in my spirit.' Rather, they came to hear Jesus speak to them."

I said that if they could not give a direct prophetic word from God, to stop with the impressions and their own thoughts and feelings! Even if those feelings were motivated by the Holy Spirit, until the words, "My child ... says the Lord," come out, all you are sharing are your interpretations of what God is saying.

I am laboring this point because the shift in anointing is incredible when you get this right.

When you speak on behalf of God instead of interpreting for God, the power comes down. Watch for that earthquake!

So, when the Lord gives you revelation, speak it out as a decree. It is during this time that I often see a messenger angel in the spirit bringing me a scroll. I may even be standing before the Father and He hands me a signet ring or a scroll.

The Power of Release

When I see that, I know that He is giving me a word to speak. The Father sees the full picture. He is the one who has the pattern. When you take that pattern from His hand, feel the weight of it because it is not for you to hold. It is for you to establish.

There is no greater accomplishment for a prophet than to release the will of God into the earth, and to send forth words that will not return void, but indeed accomplish that for which they were sent.

We will overcome, if we allow ourselves to be positioned and go through the process to be positioned. That is when the fresh revelation will come. You will no longer be breaking ground but speaking forth decrees.

The Prophetic Construction Site

I absolutely love the finality and security of decree. When you are positioned on the foundation of a birthed mandate, you stand as a foreman on a construction site. Every word of decree you speak forth is another action that establishes, builds and sets that pattern into place.

If you want to see the Church being established as a city in this earth as it is established in heaven, then get positioned in the Throne Room and you will see it.

Just imagine for a moment, the authority and power we would experience in the Church, if we all did this. Imagine if we all took time to release God's plan on this earth. We would bring change with our biggest weapon of all - our big mouths! (Some prophetic humor there!)

> WHEN YOU ARE POSITIONED ON THE FOUNDATION OF A BIRTHED MANDATE, YOU STAND AS A FOREMAN ON A CONSTRUCTION SITE.

Never forget it. We are loud and proud, and we know how to use that noise! It is time that we use it correctly so that we may accomplish what we were put on this earth to accomplish.

The Nitty-Gritty of Decree

Remember, it is only when we have birthed that the decree follows.

> ***Isaiah 55:11*** *So shall My word be that goes forth from My mouth; it shall not return to Me void, but it shall accomplish what I please, and it shall prosper in the thing for which I sent it.*

Decree grows the baby up and puts armor on that child. It puts the words in its mouth and makes the baby's arms strong. Decree arranges the circumstances so that the road opens.

It is fine and well that I birthed the new move, and God brought these mighty warriors. Yet, they still need to be equipped and set free of demons.

The Lord knows how much they need to be set free of demons...

They also need to be set free of hurts from the past and their circumstances need to come in line.

God's people may be called and willing to come out of the wilderness. They may even be prepared to take up the position of their call, but their circumstances, children, spouse, and church, need to come in line. This is done with decree. Suddenly, you understand decree.

You know this if you are in office. You have been speaking those words forth. The Holy Spirit comes upon you, you get the word, and you speak it forth into someone's life.

The Equipping Power of Decree

I pray that God raises up more like this, who would birth, travail, and decree.

We need to decree the armor, equipping, and swords. We need to decree circumstances into line continually.

"I release those finances. I open that door. I close that door. I build that up so that they can stand strong. I tear that down because it is a hindrance to them in the name of Jesus. I uproot those weeds. I plant those seeds."

The words of Jeremiah suddenly make so much sense, don't they?

Just look in the book of Lamentation - what a beautiful book of birthing and travail it is.

You cannot have one without the other. Yet, you most definitely need decree because no one abandons a newborn. It is when the child is born that the real work begins. This is when you need to speak things forth.

First you break ground. Then the birthing process creates the foundation, but the decree builds up the walls. Isn't that exciting?

Now is the time to get together with the other prophets and have your focus of what you birthed.

What is the focus?

Well, what has God given you to birth lately? Pick up from there and watch the Lord progress your vision!

Now… Step Out and Prophesy, Prophet!

You can imagine that after all that pouring out, you can feel a bit tired and dry. Those workers need encouragement to continue. Those mighty warriors who you are decreeing for, need you every now and again to walk up to them and say, "Hang in there. You are on the right track."

This applies to whichever realm God is using you in. We can do so much in the secret place, but then we need to come out of there and give people a little bit of help and encouragement to keep going. However, we are doing it backwards. We go from prophecy to decree and then wonder why we don't do any spiritual birthing.

Let's make this track nice and straight! Have you ever wondered why the first thing that God does when He calls a prophet is to put them in obscurity?

DON'T YOU UNDERSTAND THAT BY THE TIME YOU GIVE THAT PROPHETIC WORD, YOU SHOULD ALREADY HAVE BROKEN GROUND, SOWN THE SEEDS, AND PULLED THE WEEDS?

How many of you women, have given birth in a public square? How many women went to a shopping mall to give birth, where there was an audience?

You do not want everybody there. It is the same spiritually. So, what does God do the minute He calls a prophet and they reach prophetic office?

He draws you aside into the quiet so that you might birth. Then, after you birth, you can decree, and from there, step out of that season with a word of prophecy for the Church.

Once you have broken ground, birthed, and decreed, you are in a much better place to give solid words of prophecy from the Throne Room! How many prophets go to the Throne Room long enough to just get a prophetic word?

They do not do any spiritual heavy lifting. Then they wonder why the prophetic word they gave did not come to pass.

Don't you understand that by the time you give that prophetic word, you should already have broken ground, sown the seeds, and pulled the weeds?

Be Accountable!

When I look at someone and want to know if they are a real prophet or not, I want to know, "How much do you travail?"

I want to know how much time you spend in travail to qualify you to prophesy to me. Don't come and give me your "blah blah" prophetic word, if you did not travail that word through to birth first.

Have you released and birthed God's word first? Are you qualified to stand up and blab your mouth at me?

Do you go to a doctor just because he says he is a good doctor and knows a few things from Wikipedia? Would you trust a doctor like that?

Decree and Prophecy From the Throne Room

Why should we trust prophets like that? Have you gone through the process and are you prophesying to me, according to what you have birthed and decreed from the Throne Room first?

If you are, then by all means, come! I could sure use the encouragement! Just do not come blabbing your mouth at me, if you have not had your moment of travail, because you will have nothing to give the Church.

All you will have are empty words that are not anointed and based on logic.

I had a lady come to me at a seminar once who did just this to me. (I promise... I was well-behaved. You would be so proud of me). I was nice and smiled, even though I did not want to. It was a test of my sanctification.

She came to me and said, "Sister, I've got a word for you."

I thought, "You are at our prophetic seminar and it is not like I am lacking prophetic words with an entire prophetic team around me." However, I said, "Sure."

"God tells me that you are going to have an international ministry. You are going to start a movement and it is apostolic."

I was like, "No!?"

Our ministry name is *Apostolic Movement International*, and it was only splashed everywhere during the workshop... I did not have the heart to state the obvious. I just said, "Thank you, my sister. That is lovely."

That was as much niceness as I could squeeze out.

Lord, save us from the "blah-blah". I am so done. I am done receiving those words and done giving those words. Let's just get on with it and change this world.

For everyone who wants to run around doing the "blah-blah"... more power to you. Knock yourself out. I am sure there is someone out there who feels like being harassed.

However, I want to leave behind an inheritance - something that remains. I don't care if anybody knows my name or sees my face.

Think of It This Way...

Do you personally know what Watchman Nee looked like? Have you attended any of his meetings?

No, but you know his name, don't you?

He spent most of his life in jail. So, how does that work?

It seems that this is a man who knew how to travail. You just need to read his books to see that he knew how to travail.

What kind of heritage do you want to leave behind?

The Prophet's Passion

I want to do something that matters in this world. God did not take us through death and fire, through losing relationships, dying on the cross, and through a stripping of everything that was important to us, so that we could just give a prophetic word.

"Lord, help me. Surely, what I went through was worth more than that. Surely, I was called to something higher."

Yes, you were. You were called to birth the plan for this end-times move, prophet! It rests upon your shoulders. You are called to bring to pass the very plan of our Heavenly Father.

You are to go to the Throne Room in boldness and take that scroll from His hand and eat it like Ezekiel did. Then, you travail because it becomes so bitter in your stomach, until that word comes to pass.

Imagine if all of us did that. We would see an accelerated change in the body of Christ.

Prophetic Prayer:

1. Breaking Ground
2. Get on the Wall
3. Pray Heaven to Earth – Enter the Throne Room
4. Spiritual Birthing
5. Spiritual Warfare
6. Decree
7. Prophecy

BONUS
PRACTICAL DO'S AND DON'TS OF PROPHETIC PRAYER

I have covered a lot of ground, but I want to end with some practical principles for you to keep in mind as you engage in prophetic prayer. Do yourself a favor and tick off the ones you already adhere to. Then, underline the ones where you feel you still need some work.

Ask yourself why you are struggling in this area and what you can do to be more effective in prophetic prayer.

DO NOT USE PROPHETIC PRAYER AS A PERSONAL PRAYER TIME

If you want to understand more about personal prayer, please read *Persistent Prayer- Angels and Demons at Work*[viii] and learn those principles first. All the principles taught here are to fulfill your prophetic office function.

So, this is not a time for, "Lord Jesus, I am so sorry for my personal sins. I am sorry that I did not listen to you yesterday on the way to work. I know that I should have gone left when I went right. Father, I bring my family to you..."

This is not a personal prayer time. If you want to have that kind of prayer time, do it before you come to prophetic prayer. You are not stepping in as mom, pops, brother, or sister. You are stepping out as a prophet in office. Act like one.

DO STAND IN **AUTHORITY**, NOT IN HYSTERICAL SHOUTING

Dwell upon this.

You are the mom, shouting hysterically, "I am so sick and tired of the mess in this house! Why won't you do what I ask? Why didn't you make your bed?"

Give the woman a tranquilizer! It hurts to listen. If other people have to pray with you, there is only so much that they can take. Chill!

When I am truly standing in my authority, I do not need to shout at the devil hysterically. I just do that when I am angry and frustrated.

When I am confident in who I am as a prophet, I stand in my authority and I do not mince my words. I am direct and to the point.

WHEN I AM TRULY STANDING IN MY AUTHORITY, I DO NOT NEED TO SHOUT AT THE DEVIL HYSTERICALLY.

I am the mom who looks deep into her ten-year-old's eyes and says, "You will pick up your shoes and you will go upstairs to your bedroom. You will make your bed, Michael. Are we clear?"

He gives me the eye, picks up his shoes very slowly, and watches to see if I am going to change my mind. I do not flinch. I have my eyebrow fully in place and stare without wavering until my glare burns into him. After he is quite sure that "mommy means business," he takes himself upstairs and makes his bed! (To be fair, he is child #4 so this mommy has had some practice!)

That is authority, people. If we can master it with our kids, then we can master it with the devil!

Big Mouth or Big Faith?

Stand in your authority. You do not need to jump around to be heard. Just because you are shouting at the devil, does not mean that he is going to listen to you. Trust me, you do not need to shout at him to make him react. You can just tell him to get lost, with faith in your words!

If I shout, it is because I am angry. It is not because I think that shouting is going to make the devil bow any more than without my raised voice. I do not need to shout to tell him to bow. He is not worth the effort. I suppose maybe it is good for cardio, but that is about it.

It is just a good workout and when you walk out of prayer you can say that you worked off a couple of calories. Your watch will probably tell you that you got some good steps in.

So, know your authority before you step into that battlefield and do not mistake angry words and over-emotion for prophetic authority.

DO STAND IN THE MANTLE OF ANOINTING

When you come to pray, I want you to be aware of the authority that God has given you as a prophet. Step into it. I know that this sounds a little strange, because it's not like you "get it" and "lose it" every five minutes. (I covered this in *Prophetic Anointing*[ix].)

However, you are not always deliberately aware of it. God has given you that office and put the authority in you. Just because you do not feel it, does not mean that it is not there.

Even as a blood-bought child of God, He has given you authority in this earth. You need to step into your prayer time fully aware of that mantle. See it on your shoulders. See the key in your hands and realize that you have been born for this purpose.

Step Into the Mantle

When you open your eyes, you are not staring at the world as #YourNameHere! You are staring at it through the eyes of Christ. You are saying, "Ok Lord, give it to me. What do you need me to do?"

You are not standing in "your" revelation and "your" authority. You are standing in His.

If you go to a prayer time with that attitude and motivation, you will feel empowered by the Holy Spirit because you will be aware of Him.

YOU ARE NOT STANDING IN "YOUR" REVELATION AND "YOUR" AUTHORITY. YOU ARE STANDING IN HIS.

You will not be so conscious of yourself, your feelings, your revelations, and your thoughts. You will put those aside and be aware of the mind of Christ. You will step into that mantle, open your eyes, and realize that you are not speaking as a mere person, but as a prophet.

I know that what I just said sounded a bit contradictory but roll with it for a moment. You are not just anybody with your own thoughts and feelings.

You are a prophet, which means that you have the mind of Christ and you will speak from His mind and not your own.

DO WHEN PRAYING WITH OTHERS, JUMP IN ONE ANOTHER'S RIVERS

When praying in a group, do not think you need to carry it singlehandedly.

Did you ever play this game as a kid? You all sat in a circle and the first person started a story and then suddenly stopped. Then the second person had to pick up where they left off and keep the story going. You continue until everyone has had a chance. The story ends up completely different than how you thought it would!

Well, that is a bit of how you should flow with others when praying as a group. If you want more unity, continue praying where the person before you ended off. In other words, if they started praying a vision through, "jump into their stream" and continue praying in the same vein.

DO NOT PRAY FAST AND FUMBLE. SPEAK CLEARLY

When I am standing in authority, I choose my words very specifically. However, I have been in more prayer meetings than I can count where someone prayed like this, "Devil, I tell you to go now, in the name of Jesus. In the name of Jesus... *Tongues*... devil, I tell you to go right now in the name of Je-s..."

They did not even get the whole word "Jesus" out. Instead they just kept saying, "In the name of Je-s."

Who is Je-s?

At least take the time to say the name "Jesus". Breathe, before you hyperventilate!

"In the name of Je-... In the name of Je..."

No... in the name of Jesus, every knee will bow!

Practical Do's and Don'ts of Prophetic Prayer

If you are fumbling over your words because you are praying so fast that you are just throwing words out there, then I do not want to pray with you! Sorry guys, it just had to be said. Those "machine gun" prayer warriors are intense, and it is hard to jump into their stream because you cannot catch half of what they are saying.

Being in a prayer meeting with someone like that is uncomfortable. I am trying so hard not to judge, but yet silently I am, and I think to myself, "It sounds painful. I do not think that I could keep up. I am just thankful that God can hear your heart, because I do not even know if His ears can keep up with that. Calm down! You are not speaking in authority. You are speaking in emotion."

> THOSE "MACHINE GUN" PRAYER WARRIORS ARE INTENSE, AND IT IS HARD TO JUMP INTO THEIR STREAM BECAUSE YOU CANNOT CATCH HALF OF WHAT THEY ARE SAYING.

So, if you are nervous or have just developed the habit of being a "machine gun prophet" then stop and take a breath. Take your time. It is alright. The others in the group can just wait for you to get done! Bind the devil, if you have to bind him. Release the power, if you need to release the power. Yet, please do it so that everyone else understands what you are saying.

DO NOT QUIT WHEN THE LULL COMES

If you stop right there, then all you did was clean up from yesterday. You have not started to birth yet, and the next day you are just going to be cleaning up again. You may see some change in your circumstances, but you won't see the pattern really manifest in your life, as God promised.

Remember, when you get to that "quiet" after praying for a bit, you are transitioning into the Throne Room! Now is the time to either birth or do spiritual warfare.

DO STOP ONCE THE DECREE HAS GONE OUT

This is a hard one, because this is where it gets really exciting. Once you finally give out that decree, you are positioned in the Throne Room, your faith is soaring, and the power is tangible. You want to go wild but actually, your job is done.

Good, you feel fantastic. Go do a workout or something. Go for a walk.

Come on, you are pumped because you have been in the presence of the Lord. So, go and do something great. If you have the opportunity, prophesy over someone or go and speak a word of encouragement over a church!

For me, I go and write a book. What do you do?

DO NOT USE THE WORD AGAINST THE LORD

"Lord, your Word says…"

"You don't say? I did not know that about *MY* Word."

Use the Word Against the Enemy

Use the Word against your circumstances and against the enemy. I got that lovely principle from one of my spiritual kids, Anja Sager. I thought it was so brilliant because we make that mistake all the time.

"Lord, your Word says that the enemy will come against me one way and flee before me seven ways."

God knows that. He gave you the Word to use against the enemy. Why are you throwing it back at Him?

"Satan, the Word of God says that you will flee before me seven ways. You be gone."

I am standing in my authority and on the Word. Now, come in line."

Use the Word to Bring Circumstances in Line

"For you are of God, little children and have overcome them. For greater is He that is in you than he that is in the world.

Satan, greater is He that is in me. Bow!"

"Circumstances, the Word of God tells me that I am above and not beneath, the head and not the tail. It says that I will be blessed in the city and in the country. Do you hear the Word of God, circumstances?"

THE WORD IS A WEAPON… USE IT! IF GOD GIVES YOU A SCRIPTURE, HE DOES NOT INTEND FOR YOU TO THROW IT BACK AT HIM.

See, now you are using the Word as a sword and not just throwing it back at God. This is so much more effective than playing "scripture tag" with the Lord.

The Lord gives you a scripture and you are so excited about it that you throw it back at Him. I can imagine Him thinking, "They are not getting it."

So, He throws another scripture to you and you say, "Yes, God your Word says…" You just throw it back to Him again.

The cheeky side of me imagines the Lord looking down at us thinking, "Seriously though, guys!?"

The Word is a weapon… use it! If He gives you a scripture, He does not intend for you to throw it back at Him. He intends for you to use it against your circumstance, the problem, or the enemy.

DO NOT JUST QUOTE SCRIPTURES AND CALL THAT PRAYER

If you stand there quoting scripture after scripture and then say, "I had a good time of decree…." This was not prayer. This would be called quoting scriptures.

It sounds like you had a good bible study. I love having bible studies, but do not call it prayer. This is a common mistake for people who do not know how to pray effectively. They pick a ton of scriptures that back up their request and throw them around for an hour or so. They declare the logos Word and while the Word of God is indeed powerful, it is a weapon to be used coupled with decree and revelation to be effective in prayer.

Use the Word as a sword and then continue in prayer and decree.

DO NOT BE APOLOGETIC FOR YOUR REVELATION

I am not saying that you are always going to get it right. In fact, at the beginning, you will probably mess things up. Your revelation may be off the wall and you may be in complete deception.

I promise, you are not going to go to hell if you miss it or make a mistake. God is so gracious. He did not pick you out of the pit and save you from your trials, just to disown you because you mess it up once or twice.

Come now, let us have a little bit more faith in our Father than that. Let us have all grace with which we may serve God acceptably. Is that not what it tells us in Hebrews 12:28?

So, do not be apologetic.

"Guys, I think I have a word, but I could be wrong. I have this revelation, but please, it could be wrong."

Just spit it out! What is the revelation?

"Well, I see this door…"

That is good. Speak it out.

You faintly whisper, "In Jesus' name…"

That is the opposite of getting hysterical. Let's find a healthy middle line here, shall we?

Do not be apologetic about your revelations. Do not be apologetic for what you feel in the spirit or for what God tells you. Just say it as it is and if you are wrong, then you are wrong.

At least you did something about it. You did a lot more than many people are prepared to do. You are praying a lot more than a lot of prophets are prepared to pray.

Get on the road. Mess up. If you are in an environment where you are still learning, just let the people know that you are still learning and that you may miss it. Tell them that at the beginning of the meeting, but not before every single revelation that you get.

As someone who prays with others often, I find it frustrating if they always begin their revelation with, "I might be wrong but… ". I do not have time to hear whether you believe in your revelation or not because you are taking a step on the road and I need to take the next step. I need you to jump in and pray it through.

If you are wrong, I can let you know afterwards. However, let's keep praying and get the job done. Afterwards, we can sit down and talk about how it was, where God led us, and how we can do better next time.

DO NOT STOP TO SHARE ALL YOUR REVELATIONS

I want to add one more point regarding praying with others. This is not a time for everyone to stand and share every single one of their revelations. This is a tricky one, because you will slip into it a lot easier than you realize.

As you are busy praying, someone will finish a prayer and you will see this incredible revelation. Firstly, you get super excited about the revelation. Secondly, you do not want to just start praying because the revelation will not make sense to everyone else.

IF YOU SPEND YOUR ENTIRE TIME OF PRAYER DESCRIBING ALL YOUR VISIONS AND REVELATIONS TO EVERYONE, THEN YOU ARE NOT BRINGING HEAVEN DOWN TO EARTH. YOU ARE JUST DESCRIBING WHAT HEAVEN LOOKS LIKE.

So, you stop to share the revelation that you got. You share about the vision, what God told you, what you are feeling, what you are thinking, and... the anointing just dies. The momentum is completely lost.

Especially when you are praying in a group, you are praying one after the other and you are meant to be marching. If one person suddenly stops in mid step and spends ten minutes telling you about their vision, and the next prophet, not wanting to be outdone... spends ten minutes sharing their revelation, then you end up spending the entire time comparing visions.

If you spend your entire time of prayer describing all your visions and revelations to everyone, then you are not bringing heaven down to earth. You are just describing what heaven looks like.

You need to do something with those revelations.

DO NOT PREACH A SERMON

We have all seen it done. "And Lord, just as you taught us that it is better to give than receive, we pray, Lord, that you would open the storehouses of heaven. Convict us, Lord, to be faithful in giving as much as we have received. May we obey your Word, because we know, Lord, that you love a cheerful giver... "

You know it and I know it... that person has got an agenda! No, they are not praying to the Lord, they are trying to get their message across to you. It's just less confrontational to "pray your preach" than to say it directly to the person for whom you intended it!

The Prophet: Armed and Dangerous

Let's just get to business. Let our yes be yes and our no be no. Prayer is a weapon in the hands of the prophet and we should honor it as such. Anyone who is taught to use any form of firearm is first taught safety measures.

You do not qualify to shoot a firearm at a firing range until you follow safety protocol. The same is to be said for prophetic prayer. What we do in the spirit has the power to change the course of a nation, guys. Recognize that as you break ground, birth, and release, things will change!

So, just like you would not idly point and shoot bullets into the air, do not idly throw around your words. Pray with intent. Recognize what the Lord has given to you.

I hope that as you go over these principles of prophetic prayer again that you can pick out the points that are relevant to you. I have shared a lot of this from the Word, our ministry experience, and what the Lord has shown me through the years.

So then, all that is left to be said is, where is your portion of the wall, prophet?

How well is the ground broken up? Have you birthed the focus God has given to you? Good! Now decree and before all is said and done, do not forget as you leave the Throne Room to prophesy some of that heaven down to earth!

[viii] Toach, Colette. *Persistent Prayer: Angels and Demons at Work.* San Diego, California: Apostolic Movement International LLC, 2020

[ix] Toach, Colette. *Prophetic Anointing: Anointed to Worship.* Prophetic Field Guide Series, Vol. 3. 2nd ed. San Diego, California: Apostolic Movement International LLC, 2016

ABOUT THE AUTHOR

Born in Bulawayo, Zimbabwe and raised in South Africa, Colette had a zeal to serve the Lord from a young age. Coming from a long line of Christian leaders and having grown up as a pastor's kid, she is no stranger to the realities of ministry. Despite having to endure many hardships such as her parents' divorce, rejection, and poverty, she continues to follow after the Lord passionately. Overcoming these obstacles early in her life has built a foundation of compassion and desire to help others gain victory in their lives.

Since then, the Lord led Colette, with her husband, Craig Toach, to establish *Apostolic Movement International* and *Toach Ministries International*

Apostolic Movement International focuses on training those called to the fivefold ministry whereas *Toach Ministries International* ministers to, covers, supports, and spiritually parents like-minded leaders.

In addition, Colette is a fantastic cook, an amazing mom to not only her four natural children, but to her numerous spiritual children all over the world. Colette is also a renowned author, mentor, trainer, and a woman that has great taste in shoes! The scripture to "be all things to all men" definitely applies to her, and the Lord keeps adding to that list of things each and every day.

How does she do it all? Experience through every book and teaching the life of an apostle firsthand and get the insight into how the call of God can make every aspect of your life an incredible adventure.

OTHER BOOKS BY COLETTE TOACH

If you enjoyed this book, I know you will also love the following books.

Persistent Prayer

Angels and Demons at Work

ISBN: 978-1-62664-225-6

Prayer is our connection to the Lord. It takes the will of God in heaven and brings it down to the earth. It removes the hindrances that stand in the way, allows man to hear God, and blocks the enemy completely! When you couple this with someone who is ready to speak, obey, and do the will of God in this earth, you get a recipe for a highly successful prayer life.

Strategies of War

Battle Plans for the Modern Day Christian

ISBN: 978-1-62664-112-9

No more allowing the enemy to have his way. Take back your land and remove him from your life for good.

Your victory is at hand. So, take hold and allow Colette Toach to guide and teach you the strategy to tearing down the kingdom of darkness.

Prophetic Anointing

Anointed to Worship

Book 3 of the Prophetic Field Guide Series

ISBN: 978-1-62664-094-8

God has promised you a visit to the Throne Room! This is your summons from Almighty God. It is time for you to experience Him face-to-face and heart-to-heart. Get ready for the meeting of a lifetime. It is time to flow in the anointing in ways you have never known to be possible.

FURTHER RECOMMENDATIONS BY THE AUTHOR

Earn a Diploma That Truly Validates Your Call

With over twenty years' experience in full-time ministry, Apostles Craig and Colette Toach know the fire that burns in you to do the work of God.

With a focus on spiritual parenting, mentorship, and hands-on training, each school equips you to do the work of God. Consider us boot camp for your fivefold ministry call.

Each course is video based with required report submissions for you to complete after each lesson. Each student is allocated a trainer who marks all reports, follows up with personal ministry, and laying on of hands at graduation.

AMI Prophetic School:

www.prophetic-school.com

There is a clear track that the Holy Spirit follows to train up His prophets. Having trained prophets into office all over the world, your calling will find itself in an environment where your prophetic mandate is as important to us as it is to you.

Think: training, impartation, and mentorship. By the time you walk the stage at your graduation, you would have done more than just studied for a diploma – you would have embarked on a journey that would have equipped you to fulfill your mandate as a prophet in office.

AMI Pastor Teacher School:

www.pastorteacherschool.com

Everything you wish you knew about doing the work of the ministry. Our student complement consists of pastors, ministry leaders, apostles, and various fivefold ministers who crave a deeper reality of the Lord and their calling.

With an emphasis on becoming equipped, each course gears you towards functioning in a leadership capacity. Whether that is behind the pulpit or in a home church setting, you will receive training that by the time you walk the stage, would have already geared you towards apostolic ministry.

AMI Campus:

www.ami-campus.com

Not ready to commit to a lengthy training program? No problem! You are welcome to study independently and pick and choose between prophetic, pastoral, teaching, and apostolic courses that tailor fit you right where you are at.

The main difference between our public campus and our other schools is that associates in our campus do not graduate, but rather join a family of like-minded believers. Every associate is supported by qualified pastors and guided through their individual training process. We are here to see your process through!

Colette Toach's books are now available on both, Kindle and iBooks!

REACH OUT!

Find out More Here:
www.colette-toach.com

Connect with Colette Toach on Facebook!
www.facebook.com/ColetteToach

Check Colette out on Amazon.com at:
www.amazon.com/author/colettetoach

Connect with Craig and Colette Toach Personally:
www.toach-ministries.com

Get Colette's books at AMI Bookshop: www.ami-bookshop.com

Telephone: +1 (760) 466 - 7679

(9am to 5pm California Time, Tuesday – Saturday)

E-mail Address: admin@ami-bookshop.com

BIBLIOGRAPHY

Toach, Colette. *The Way of Dreams and Visions: Interpreting Your Secret Conversion with God.* 3rd ed. San Diego, California: Apostolic Movement International LLC, 2016

Toach, Colette. *Persistent Prayer: Angels and Demons at Work.* San Diego, California: Apostolic Movement International LLC, 2020

Toach, Colette. *Prophetic Field Guide Series.* Vol. 1-7. San Diego, California: Apostolic Movement International LLC, 2014 - 2016

Toach, Colette. *Prophetic Anointing: Anointed to Worship.* Prophetic Field Guide Series, Vol. 3. 2nd ed. San Diego, California: Apostolic Movement International LLC, 2016

Toach, Colette. *Prophetic Warrior: Weapon Training for the Prophet at Arms.* Prophetic Field Guide Series, Vol. 5. 2nd ed. San Diego, California: Apostolic Movement International LLC, 2016

Toach, Colette. *Strategies of War: Battle Plans for the Modern Day Christian.* 2nd ed. San Diego, California: Apostolic Movement International LLC, 2017